KILLING CA

How to Destroy a Perfectly Good Theology from the Inside

Greg Dutcher
Cruciform Press | Released June, 2012

To Roscoe Adams
November 19, 1943 – April 22, 2012

The most joyful, humble, and gracious Calvinist I've ever known. While I have many teachers, I have few spiritual fathers. Thank you for the privilege of being your true son in the faith.

You were alive and well when this dedication was first written, but you never saw it because God wanted you to see something far superior—and you're seeing it. I'll see it with you on the other side.

– Greg Dutcher

"This book blew me away! Greg Dutcher skillfully diagnoses how I kill the very truth I love by my hypocrisy, pride, anger, and judgmental attitude. This book will serve a young generation of Calvinists. But the older generation had better heed it, too. There's medicine here for all our hearts, and taking this medicine will make us more joyful and more humble when making our glorious God known."

Thabiti Anyabwile, author; Senior Pastor, First Baptist Church, Grand Cayman; Council Member, The Gospel Coalition

"Many Calvinists will find reading this book to be a painful experience. But medicine is like that. The good news is that a healthy dose of Dutcher's wisdom will go a long way in bringing spiritual health to the young, restless, and reformed."

Sam Storms, author, speaker; Senior Pastor of Bridgeway Church, Oklahoma City

"An absolute must-read for every YRR—and older Calvinists too! With wit, compassion, and candor, Greg Dutcher exposes how sin taints our theological convictions and undermines our witness. But he doesn't leave us there; through biblical and historical examples he shows us Calvinism done right to the glory of God."

Lydia Brownback, author and speaker

Table of Contents

Introduction 5

Chapters

One   *By Loving Calvinism as an End in Itself* 13

Two   *By Becoming a Theologian Instead of a Disciple* 23

Three   *By Loving God's Sovereignty More Than God Himself* 35

Four   *By Losing an Urgency in Evangelism* 47

Five   *By Learning Only from Other Calvinists* 59

Six   *By Tidying Up the Bible's "Loose Ends"* 69

Seven   *By Being an Arrogant Know-It-All* 79

Eight   *By Scoffing at the Hang-ups Others Have with Calvinism.* 93

Afterword 105
No Book Can Save Calvinism

Appendix. 106
The Calvinist's Favorite Flower: T.U.L.I.P.

Endnotes 107

More books from Cruciform Press. 112

CruciformPress
something new in Christian publishing

Our Books: Short. Clear. Concise. Helpful. Inspiring. Gospel-focused. *Print; ebook formats: Mobi, ePub, PDF.*

Consistent Prices: Every book costs the same.

Subscription Options: Print books or ebooks delivered to you on a set schedule, at a discount. Or buy print books or ebooks individually.

Pre-paid or Recurring Subscriptions
Print Book . . . . $6.49 each
Ebook . . . . $3.99 each

Non-Subscription Sales
1-5 Print Books . . . . $8.45 each
6-50 Print Books . . . . $7.45 each
More than 50 Print Books . . . . $6.45 each
Single Ebooks (bit.ly/CPebks) . . . . $5.45 each

CruciformPress.com

Killing Calvinism: How to Destroy a Perfectly Good Theology from the Inside

Print / PDF ISBN: 978-1-936760-53-4
ePub ISBN: 978-1-936760-55-8
Mobipocket ISBN: 978-1-936760-54-1

Published by Cruciform Press, Adelphi, Maryland. Copyright © 2012 by Greg Dutcher. All rights reserved. Unless otherwise indicated, all Scripture quotations are taken from: The Holy Bible: English Standard Version, Copyright © 2001 by Crossway Bibles, a division of Good News Publishers. Used by permission. All rights reserved. Italics or bold text within Scripture quotations indicates emphasis added.

INTRODUCTION

It's interesting to compare the typical Calvinist of yesteryear with his 21st-century counterpart. The former favored his tweed sport coat and may very well have been caught taking out the garbage while wearing a necktie. The latter prefers ripped jeans and sandals, and on any given Sunday may be found serving communion in the same outfit. The Calvinist of old attended worship services in a stately spired church building; lived in a quiet, well-kept home; and enjoyed listening to Bach on his phonograph. Could he have gazed down the corridors of time, he would have stared incredulously at today's 20-something Calvinist dancing madly in total silence, some kind of white wires dangling from his ears as he prepares to attend a meeting of his missional church in a dingy *YMCA*. Yesterday's Calvinist discussed the finer points of Berkhoff's *Systematic Theology* with his button-down peers at the Philadelphia Conference of Reformed Theology; the hipster Calvinist kicks around a little Grudem and Driscoll at the local sports bar over a pint of Guinness.

Ridiculous generalizations? Sure, but I trust you see my point. Calvinism is "in" right now, and while it struts about in different dress than it did, say, a century ago, it has the same theological framework that propelled men from Augustine to Piper to impact the world with their writing and teaching. While Calvinism itself has not changed,[1] it has attracted a distinctly contemporary audience. Charles Spurgeon noticed this same continuity of doctrine but freshness of expression in his day:

> It is no novelty, then, that I am preaching; no new doctrine. I love to proclaim these strong old doctrines that are called by the nickname Calvinism, but which are surely and verily the revealed truth of God as it is in Christ Jesus. By this truth I make a pilgrimage into the past, and as I go, I see father after father, confessor after confessor, martyr after martyr, standing up to shake hands with me …. Taking these things to be the standard of my faith, I see the land of the ancients peopled with my brethren—I behold multitudes who confess the same as I do, and acknowledge that this is the religion of God's own church.[2]

Had Spurgeon done a 180 and seen the future of the church, particularly the early part of the 21st century, he would have found an equally enthusiastic group of confessors as he saw in church history. And he may have been stunned at the army of young preachers in novelty Ts and hipster glasses who regard him as nothing less than a Victorian rock star.

Today, many Reformed Christians joyfully communicate the great doctrines of grace to a young, attention-challenged group (did you notice how short this book is?). And though it seems as unlikely as middle-schoolers starting Shakespeare study groups, the generation shaped by graphic novels and unlimited texting has risen up to embrace a high view of God, and this will inevitably shape the doctrinal future of contemporary evangelicalism. While I am a little older than most of my "Young, Restless, and Reformed" peers, I enthusiastically stand with them in this unique moment in church history.[3] In doing so, I hope to offer a small contribution that may help us all not to kill off our Calvinism.

From a Portal to a Bunker

I became a Christian in 1986 at age 16, entering the kingdom through a charismatic/Pentecostal portal in woodsy, semi-rural Maryland. My young faith was nurtured by a bizarre amalgamation of Christian rock, cheesy 70s movies about believers vanishing from the earth en masse, and Jack Chick tracts—those pictures of cartoon sinners burning in the lake of fire will stay with me a lifetime. While this does give me an edge at parties when the talk drifts toward unusual conversions and odd formative experiences, the fact is I was a theological train wreck. Yet the grace of God proved greater than my personal and theological deficiencies, and providence kept leading me into a greater and greater appreciation for God's Word.

By 1989 I had discovered the verse-by-verse Bible teaching of John MacArthur, and I simply could not get enough. I spent every dime I had on sermon tapes (yes, plastic cassettes larger than my current cell phone). Every now and then, MacArthur would mention something about "divine election" or "predestination," and it always made me shudder. In college by this time, I told some of my friends, "MacArthur's a great teacher if you leave out that Calvinism thing."

But then there was Tim, an outspoken advocate for this strange-sounding doctrine. For months he challenged me on the issue of God's sovereignty in salvation. I will never forget the day he said to me, "Dutcher, do you think anybody *deserves* to be in heaven?"

"Of course not," I replied.

"Then why are you so bent out of shape if some people get grace and everyone else gets what they deserve? Nobody's getting shafted," Tim reasoned.

I rolled my eyes and blew it off …on the outside. But Tim's question placed a stone in my shoe that I simply could not remove. Eventually, I picked up R. C. Sproul's book *Chosen by God*, and it was all over. He had me halfway through the first chapter. Interestingly, my "switch" to Calvinism was very similar to Sproul's take on his own conversion: "Reluctantly, I sighed and surrendered, but with my head, not my heart. 'OK, I believe this stuff, but I don't have to like it!'"[4] I will come back to Dr. Sproul's transparency later in this book, but I suspect that many "newborn" Calvinists likely start their journey on a similar note.

Before too long, my reluctant acceptance of Calvinism-writ-large matured into a genuine love for the doctrines of grace. I realized that God's love for me was so great that he had my eternal well-being deep in his eternal heart long before I came on the scene. I also came to see that my sinfulness was so horrible, so debilitating to all of my faculties, that without God outright saving me, apart from any cooperation on my part, I was doomed to everlasting judgment. Paul's words in Romans 9:16, once an unsettling "anomaly" in my ill-formed theology, now became an oasis of peace and confidence: "So then it depends not on human will or exertion, but on God, who has mercy." What rest! I was saved and preserved completely on the basis of God's proactive kindness.

Like many fresh-from-the-factory Calvinists, I could not wait to share my newfound understanding of God's mercy, salvation, and sovereignty with others. How odd it was, then, to find that so many friends did not share my enthusiasm. *Perhaps*, I thought, *I just need share my own struggle in coming to a Reformed perspective.* But that almost never worked. "Oh, I see. I haven't arrived like you have, right Greg?" Like Sisyphus, the more I pushed my T.U.L.I.P.-engraved boulder up the hill, the more it rolled back on me. Eventually, I made the dreaded mistake I fear many Calvinists continue to make today: I looked for the bunker instead of the coffee shop.

The bunker is the place of uniformity and safety. It is comfortable; it feels like home. In the bunker, we can be ourselves, accepted for who we are, because we are a lot like everyone around us. But the coffee shop, in this analogy, is the place where you at least have a possibility of engaging in meaningful conversation with someone who doesn't quite believe what you believe. Such a coffee shop can be fairly comfortable, but it's not home. It is the public square, and it is full of people who don't think like you do.

I sometimes fear that if we all just stay holed up in our bunkers, we will end up killing the revival of Calvinism in our midst. I dread the thought of my kids and grandkids looking back decades from now at this time and concluding that Calvinism was merely the flavor of the month. If the theology of Augustine, Calvin, Knox, Edwards, Spurgeon, and Piper has been able to strengthen the church, advance the gospel, and protect Christians from the damnable influences of false gospels, then you and I must do all we can to make sure that what's going on right now is more than just a fad. We must not give current and future generations plausible reasons to reject the very essence of Christianity that we believe Calvinism represents.

That is, if we don't live our Calvinism, we might just kill it.

Consider the harm we Calvinists can do to ourselves, our spouses, our children, and ultimately our legacies if we do not think, meditate, pray, preach, and practice our Calvinism—our *faith*—as we should. How can anyone believe that this body of doctrine is ultimately sound and biblical if it has only an academic effect on many of its proponents? What areas of our lives should be transformed as a direct result of what we believe and embrace? What areas should *not* be? Shouldn't Calvinism be able to do more than provide us with a potent arsenal for debating an Arminian? Shouldn't it do more than establish a set of technical terms by which we can join the Calvinist bunker down the street?

A PhD in Blundering

In the more than twenty years since "switching sides," I have made my fair share of blunders. To my shame, I have literally made others cry with my lack of tact. At times my arrogance and insensitivity have burned like jet fuel, while I smugly justified it all because I was "standing up for the truth." I have damaged friendships, ruined Bible studies, strained prayer meetings, and actually mocked people who could not come to terms with what I believe to be true.

Meanwhile, I find myself today in a special place. The church I planted eight years ago and still pastor is non-denominational. While the church has a thoroughly Reformed flavor in its teaching, many in my congregation are not Calvinists. Some, I suspect, don't even know what Calvinism is. As a result, I have many "coffee shop" moments and have learned a great deal about how important it is to be winsome and charitable in our presentation of Reformed theology.

More importantly, I am a husband and father of four, and I am still learning how my Calvinism can be utterly wasted in my own home if not lived and handled carefully.

All this to say that I feel qualified to write this book. From my little bunker, I plead with my brothers and sisters: may we never be guilty of killing Calvinism.

While I could offer countless ways to squander the enormous potential for good in Calvinism, I have boiled them down to eight in this book. I urge you to read carefully, asking yourself often if a particular killer of Calvinism could be at work in your life right now. Most of all, I pray that your God-centered understanding of Christianity will truly impact your life with God-centered thinking, actions, and affections.

Christ is worthy of lives well lived. May he help us do just that!

One
BY LOVING CALVINISM AS AN END IN ITSELF

A few years ago, Lisa and I took our four children on a day trip to Cunningham Falls State Park in Western Maryland. As we were leaving, a kind, elderly gentleman urged us not to head back toward Baltimore until we got a good look at the sky on what promised to be a crystal clear evening. "You'll never be able to see such a pretty sight back in the city with all that haze and light pollution blocking your view," he warned us. We gladly took his advice, stopping at a Dairy Queen drive-through and finding the nearest overlook off Route 70. We sat there in the fading light, finishing our cones, talking and anticipating the natural beauty we were about to behold. As dusk settled in, however, so did our grip on reality: we realized we wouldn't have been able to see a meteor shooting ten feet away because we were looking through the smudged windshield of a well-used minivan belonging to a family with four small children.

Fortunately, with a little glass cleaner from the glove compartment and the roll of paper towels no family minivan should ever be without, Lisa was able to remove years of nasty film formed by the mysterious substances of childhood. In minutes the glass was so clean that it blended imperceptibly with the world just outside. As the darkness of a summer evening fell, our family was mesmerized by the stunning splendor of a full moon, vivid in the western Maryland sky and set among what seemed like twice as many stars as there ought to be. We sat in speechless awe as the heavens declared God's glory.

And not once did anyone say, "What a beautifully clear windshield!"

Who Praises a Windshield?

Windshields are one of those technological wonders we have all gotten used to. In fact, they work best when you don't notice them, when they are invisible so that all you can see is what they reveal.

I am concerned that many Calvinists today do little more than celebrate how wonderfully clear their theological windshield is. But like a windshield, Reformed theology is not an end in itself. It is simply a window to the awe-inspiring universe of God's truth, filled with glory, beauty, and grace. Do we need something like a metaphorical windshield of clear, biblical truth to look through as we hope to marvel at God's glory? Absolutely. But we must make sure that we know the difference between staring *at* a windshield and staring *through* one.

When I was in seminary, some friends and I went

to a theology symposium near Philadelphia where one speaker "rocked the house," to borrow a current phrase. He spoke on the glory of God as the reason we were created. With verse after verse, illustration after illustration, he thundered from the pulpit and filled our minds with powerful thoughts of God's holiness and transcendence. I remember feeling small and thinking, *Yes, this is good— I **should** feel small. It's all about God—not me!* During the break that followed, my friends and I gathered in a corner, buzzing from the message. Most of us didn't even care that we were consuming bad instant coffee and stale pastries.

"Okay, I'm ready to hear from a Calvinist now," said one friend I will call …Calvin. He was referring to the renowned Reformed theologian slated to speak next.

"Calvin, didn't you enjoy what you just heard?" someone asked.

"Yeah, he was okay, I guess. But he's no Calvinist," Calvin shrugged.

We all muttered in agreement and returned to our seats. The famous Calvinist spoke next, and he did a good job, but it seemed a bit too academic to me. He was clearly teaching sound, biblical doctrine, but it was not easy to follow him. At the next break, Calvin went on and on about how much he had enjoyed that message and how just *knowing* the speaker was a Calvinist had put him at ease.

I cannot judge my friend's heart, but I suspect many of us have come to love Reformed theology simply because it is Reformed theology. Consider your books.

We Calvinists love books, don't we? How much money have we spent on commentaries and systematic theologies just because they are Reformed in tone? Rarely have I thought, "Oh, this will help me relish the glory of God and the beauty of salvation!" I have simply laid another volume on my growing Calvinist stack. They look so good in my bookcase! Kevin DeYoung captures some of these trendier aspects of Calvinism among growing numbers of young people:

> Here are the two most important things you need to know about the rise of the New Calvinism: it's not new and it's not about Calvin. Of course, some of the conferences are new. The John Piper–packed iPods are new. The neo-reformed blog blitz is new. The ideas, however, are not. "Please God, don't let the young, restless, and reformed movement be another historically ignorant, self-absorbed, cooler-than-thou fad."[5]

All around the world blogs, study groups, conferences, podcasts, and unusual little publishing houses are churning out material on election, justification, covenantalism, ammillennialism, postmillennialism, Christo-centric hermeneutics, Augustine, Calvin, Luther and, yes, even the differences between infra-, supra- and sub-lapsarianism. Frankly, it is indeed cool to be a Calvinist right now, and more resources are available to the "Young, Restless, and Reformed" crowd than ever before. Don't get me wrong: I celebrate this resurgence and hope to see it flourish. Yet we should be careful to make sure that we are not busy polishing windshields just to mutually admire each other's techniques.

Loving Calvinism for its own sake, even with all of its rich internal language and traditions, is the fast track to killing it. There is a better way.

Through a Windshield, Clearly

Sitting there in our messy family minivan on that summer night, not only relishing what I was seeing in the sky, but also aware that this was a supremely teachable moment for our kids, I did what any loving Christian father would have done. I got our children's attention and instructed them to look closely at the windshield mommy had worked so hard at cleaning, not even leaving any streaks. I showed them the Windex, warning them against cheap substitutes, and passed along some wisdom about selecting from among the many varieties of paper towels. "If you don't understand these things," I admonished, "the sky will be obscured." Right?

No, I didn't really do any of that. I ignored the windshield. In fact, it completely vanished from my awareness. I was taken up entirely with the wonders of God's creation and the privilege of sharing this moment with my family. Emphasizing the windshield under those circumstances might make a good Monty Python skit, but it would have missed the point entirely.

The apostle Paul, often called the proto-Calvinist, taught *about* God in ways that never looked *away from* God. He spared no effort in describing the beauty, complexity, and justice of God's sovereign right to rule over all of history. Because Paul's system of doctrine was a clear windshield, he could see through it to the soul-stirring depths of God's very character.

"Oh, the depth of the riches and wisdom and knowledge of God! How unsearchable are his judgments and how inscrutable his ways!" (Romans 11:33). When Paul reflected on the doctrines that make up what we call Calvinism, he was moved to rejoice in God. This is the key to not killing off today's Calvinist upsurge. When we read our books, attend our conferences, and "Piper-up" our iPods, the primary goal must not be to gain a better understanding of 16th- and 17th-century doctrine. It must be to be blown out of the water by the God who has chosen us in infinite mercy and wisdom.

It seems that the Calvinist heroes of church history knew how to do this. They stared *through* Calvinism to get the best view of God's splendor and the gospel's glory. Charles Spurgeon fought both non-Calvinists and hyper-Calvinists in 19th-century England, but not for the sake of Calvinism per se. The former found Calvinism offensive; the latter saw it as a mandate for not preaching the free offer of the gospel to all men. Spurgeon responded to both by claiming that Calvinism is just a convenient nickname for the gospel.

In fact, Spurgeon believed that it is not possible to preach Christ and him crucified unless we preach what is called Calvinism. He meant that we cannot preach the gospel without preaching certain "Calvinistic" doctrines:

> I do not believe we can preach the gospel, if we do not preach justification by faith, without works;

nor unless we preach the sovereignty of God in
his dispensation of grace; nor unless we exalt the
electing, unchangeable, eternal, immutable, conquering love of Jehovah; nor do I think we can preach
the gospel, unless we base it upon the special and
particular redemption of his elect and chosen people
which Christ wrought out upon the cross; nor can I
comprehend a gospel which lets saints fall away after
they are called, and suffers the children of God to be
burned in the fires of damnation after having once
believed in Jesus. [6]

It is interesting that Spurgeon saw the content of
his preaching as something called Calvinism. Obviously,
Reformed theology was making a resurgence in his day:
there was a trend or a movement within 19th-century
British Christendom that gladly bore the label that has
gained new popularity in our day as well. Spurgeon
identified with that movement, but not because he was
interested in fashions. It's clear that what supremely
interested him was "Christ and him crucified," and he
allied himself with Calvinism because it was supremely
interested in the same thing. Yet, it appears that Spurgeon
never felt he was called to preach Calvinism as an end in
itself. His commission was to preach the gospel.

Notice that what consumed the British preacher
were the component truths of the gospel. These truths
ignited Spurgeon's heart and pushed him back into the
pulpit each week to preach to thousands. For Spurgeon,
the life-transforming truths of the gospel were rivet-

ing. Was he an unflinching Calvinist? Certainly. But his Calvinism was merely a way to see, appreciate, and present the glorious message of Jesus Christ and him crucified. About a century before Spurgeon, one of his heroes, George Whitefield—an avowed Calvinist—expressed a very similar view: "It is an undoubted truth that every doctrine that comes from God, leads to God; and that which doth not tend to promote holiness is not of God."[7] Whitefield saw no benefit to doctrine—even the most robust, Reformed doctrine—unless it "leads to God" and would "promote holiness."

The non-Calvinist may not discern why anyone would get excited about the Westminster Divines, the Arminian remonstrance, or the history of English Puritanism—but salvation by faith and God's unchanging, conquering love? "Yeah, I guess I can see why you guys are pumped about all of that," say the onlookers. The best Calvinists that history has given to us were using Reformed theology to get a clearer hold on the majesty of God, the wonder of the gospel, and the exhilaration of Christian living. By God's grace—yes, his sovereign grace—may we do the same.

※ ※ ※

Lord, help me not to love Calvinism as an end in itself.

Mighty God,

Thank you for giving me eyes, ears, memory, and intellect. You have enabled me to see the wonder of your sovereign mercy throughout your Word. Had you not chosen me, I would not be your child. Had you not loved me first, never would I have loved you at all.

May I never be more enamored with the theology that helps me see these things clearly than with seeing you. Forgive me for the times when I have made my understanding of you and your saving ways an idol rather than an aid. When others see me, may they see a person completely captivated by your glory and humbled by your mercy.

For Jesus' sake, amen.

Two
BY BECOMING A THEOLOGIAN INSTEAD OF A DISCIPLE

As I write this, the legendary NBA giant Shaquille O'Neal has just hung up his size-22 Reeboks after 19 years in the game. He was an impressive force on the court and will undoubtedly be heading to the Basketball Hall of Fame in due time. However, while I would never say this to his face, fans know he was a lousy free-throw shooter. Several years ago, he was found in his own gym working hours at a time trying to improve his foul shot, but as one teammate put it, "He won't let anyone read-just his basic mechanics." So while Shaq labored harder than most of his contemporaries in this area, he only succeeded in getting better and better at being consistently weak from the line.

In this respect, basketball is like most other things: if your basics are off, nothing else is really going to help you improve. And one of the great dangers of loving

Calvinism as an end in itself—as we discussed in the previous chapter—can be the unconscious redefining of one of the basics of the Christian faith: what it means to be a disciple.

A disciple is a student of Christ—someone who spends time with the Savior in order to come to know him better and resemble him more closely. As a pastor, I have found that many Christians simply assume that learning more and more about the Bible and theology— Reformed theology in particular—is *the same thing as* growing as a disciple. It isn't. Robust theology can be a powerful catalyst in this process, but like anything else, we can turn it into an idol. The danger is that, while we may begin with Reformed theology as the *framework* by which we more coherently understand and appreciate our faith, over time it can become the *substance* of our faith. At that point, daily living is more about mastering Reformed doctrine than being mastered by Jesus and his total claim over every area of life.

When does one's attention to theology become too much? It's not always easy to say. Many of the noblest aspects of genuine discipleship are often at work in those who drift this way. Discipline, study, and intellectual rigor are all commendable virtues easily found in Scripture: we say, "Do your best to present yourself to God as one approved" (2 Timothy 2:15), and "You shall love the Lord your God with all your heart and with all your soul and with all your mind" (Matthew 22:37). And we should obey such verses! The man or woman who commits to such a path is often praised for robust devotion to spiritual growth, and not without legitimate reason. But evangelical Christianity has a love affair with syrupy clichés, self-help style sound bites, and pep-talk pragmatism. We desperately need more Christians who know how to think along clear, biblical lines.[8]

But we cross a line when we are more focused on mastering theology than on being mastered by Christ.

Theology Should Serve Discipleship

While all true disciples are theologians, not all theologians are true disciples. If knowing the Bible and understanding theology were reliable measures of discipleship, Satan would be the greatest disciple ever. After all, his knowledge of Scripture is exceptional and he's been observing the spiritual realm for quite a long time.[9]

Even as the Bible exalts the value of knowledge, it warns us against the dangers of knowledge severed from love. Paul wrote, "This 'knowledge' puffs up, but love builds up …. And if I have prophetic powers, and understand all mysteries and all knowledge, and if I have all faith, so as to remove mountains, but have not love, I am nothing" (1 Corinthians 8:1; 13:2). To the extent that theological thinking is divorced from passion for the Savior and the love that is a fruit of his Holy Spirit, it falls woefully short of the grand goal of Christian living.

The most vivid picture of Christian discipleship in Scripture is that of the twelve who followed Jesus for three years: "he appointed twelve …so that *they might be with him* and *he might send them out*" (Mark 3:14).

It is interesting that Mark did not emphasize that Jesus would first *train* these men in order to send them. Rather, the emphasis is on the fact that they were simply *with* him. Discipleship is first and foremost about being with Christ. *Learning* his teaching, *following* his footsteps, and *participating* in his mission are all vital elements of discipleship, but they flow from being *in his presence*. One commentator captures this concept:

> The simple prepositional phrase "to be with him" has atomic significance in the Gospel of Mark. Discipleship is a relationship before it is a task, a "who" before a "what." If, as Genesis 3:4–5 indicates, the essence of sin is substituting a false god for the true God, being with Jesus becomes the way of forsaking human idols and honoring the true God, thus recovering the image of God (Genesis 1:26–27). To be with Jesus is the most profound mystery of discipleship. From now on his person and his work determine the existence of the Twelve.[10]

While the word disciple means "learner," it does not refer to a kind of learning that takes place primarily in a classroom. Indeed, Jesus' training method bore little resemblance to a common seminary model: daily lectures, copious notes, and a written exam as the culmination of training. I am not saying this approach is wrong; it certainly benefited me in many respects. But I am saying that Jesus understood his goal in training the Twelve was nothing short of life transformation: "A disciple is not above his teacher, but everyone who is fully trained will be like his teacher" (Luke 6:40).

Perfect training produces character change because discipleship is ultimately about resembling Christ. What is the biblical definition of a disciple? One who is becoming less like himself and more like Jesus.

And what was Jesus like? How would you describe him? Would the first words out of your mouth be, "Well, he definitely had his theology down cold. Yes, I would say that above all Jesus was an amazing theologian." Of course not. Had Jesus been an absolute master of sound biblical theology but unkind and unloving as a man, he would today be a small footnote in history.

No, although Jesus' grasp of theology was infinitely perfect in every way, what stands out the most about him is how he lived and what he did. We see this in the ways that saints have typically described him.

> Here is light to enlighten the soul, and wisdom to counsel the soul, and power to support the soul, and goodness to supply the soul, and mercy to pardon the soul, and beauty to delight the soul, and glory to ravish the soul, and fullness to fill the soul. (Thomas Brooks) [11]

> Oh, Jesus! Thy power, Thy grace, Thy justice, Thy tenderness, Thy truth, Thy majesty, and Thine immutability make up such a man, or rather such a God-man, as neither heaven nor earth hath seen elsewhere. (Charles Spurgeon) [12]

> We marvel at him because his uncompromis-
> ing justice is tempered with mercy. His majesty is
> sweetened by meekness. (John Piper) [13]

Leaving aside the qualities of Christ that are not trans-
ferable to us—immutability and divine glory, for instance[14]
—do I see such attributes growing in me? Justice, goodness,
mercy, and tenderness are all things that Jesus will repro-
duce in *everyone* who comes under his lordship. It does
not just happen occasionally. The results will look different
from one person to another, but true discipleship—even
if it includes rigorous education in theology—will always
produce a more Christlike character. Jesus did not say, "You
will know them by their mastery of doctrine."

Is it possible that too many Calvinists have been
overly reductionistic in extolling the virtues of *wisdom*
and *truth* above all other Christlike attributes? Lest you
think I am unfairly judging my Reformed brothers, let
me make a confession.

Are We of Calvin, or Christ?

I am ashamed to say that I lived a number of Christian
years more as a theologian than a disciple. My spiritual
life was rooted in one grand passion: to become a better
Calvinist. I devoured books, listened to sermons and, like
a strung-out Grateful Dead groupie, chased after every
Reformed conference I could find. My knowledge of
theology and church history skyrocketed. The highlight
of my week came whenever I had an opportunity to
stomp an Arminian to dust. When a phrase like "God

didn't make robots" or "everyone has a free will" slipped into a conversation, I could spring into action faster than a ball boy at Wimbledon. And you know what? Many of my Reformed brothers in Christ viewed me as one of the most committed Christians they knew. Because I could cross the first letter and dot the fourth letter in T.U.L.I.P, I lived under the illusion that I was a growing disciple. Little did I know that I was woefully neglecting things like mercy, kindness, and servanthood in my spiritual development.

Is it possible that it wasn't just me? Can other Calvinists be guilty of this kind of lopsided discipleship? Our knowledge of theology and church history may grow exponentially, but in radical disproportion to character change.

I know a man who is a respected elder in a Reformed church. His claim to fame is that every summer, while other vacationers are reading Grisham and King, he reads a Reformed classic. His list includes some impressive titles: Owen's *Death of Death*, Charnock's *The Existence and Attributes of God* and, of course, Calvin's *Institutes*. It's not wrong to be impressed by his commitment …and I am! In an age when many of the best-selling Christian books are, honestly, drivel, would that more Christians devoted themselves to such historical treasures!

Yet there is more to this man's story.

In addition to impressive reading habits, this man also has a notorious temper. On one disturbing occasion when he couldn't figure out how to turn off his car alarm, he started throwing every object within his reach. Yes, every Christian sins, but this kind of behavior was clearly a pattern in his life. He routinely lost his cool, even earning a nickname referring to his frequent furies. It seemed that everyone, including his fellow elders, saw his lack of self-control as novel and amusing. And it's not that he was unaware of this area in his life. Occasionally he would say, "I'm a sinner saved by grace, and I know my hot temper was forgiven at the cross." The only levelheaded response to this kind of thinking is, "Come on!" Would any of us let a serial adulterer use that excuse? Someone with a consistently foul mouth? An unrepentant alcoholic?

Such a story is an example of bad Calvinism. It reduces a system of rich truth to a set of postulates and propositions with little or no impact on how a person lives. Jesus is not impressed with our Calvin, Edwards, or Machen when we cannot grow into people of kindness and self-control. It is simply time to grow up. We need to stop killing our Calvinism.

Calvinists Should Know the End Goal Better Than Anyone

Our election to salvation comes with a guaranteed end result: "For those whom he foreknew, he also predestined to be *conformed to the image of his Son*" (Romans 8:29). In encouraging relatively new Christians at Rome, Paul links predestination not just with salvation but with sanctification—indeed with *glorification*! Piper expounds on this connection:

Our destiny to be like Christ is all about being prepared to see and savor his superiority. We must have his character and likeness to know him and see him and love him and admire him and make much of him.[15]

The Calvinist finds himself in a marvelous place. He does not have to wonder if God is fitting him for heaven. There is no mystery as to whether he will be prepared to see and savor Christ's superiority. With all respect to our non-Calvinist friends in the faith, I do not believe their doctrine permits the same measure of comfort and assurance that they will be totally ready for That Day. And once the issue of unconditional election is settled in the believer's mind, he or she is then free to find assurance of ultimate glorification in Jesus alone. The Calvinist knows that there is an elect community,[16] guaranteed of being ultimately conformed to the image of Christ, and that belonging to Jesus is ultimately the only necessary qualification. Spurgeon counseled Calvinists well regarding this ultimate question.

If you stop and say, "I want to know first whether I am elect," you ask you know not what. Go to Jesus, be you never so guilty, just as you are. Leave all curious inquiry about election alone. Go straight to Christ and hide in his wounds, and you shall know your election. The assurance of the Holy Spirit shall be given to you, so that you shall be able to say, "I know whom I have believed, and I am persuaded that he is able to keep that which I have committed to him." Christ was at the everlasting council: He can tell you whether you were chosen or not; but you cannot find it out in any other way. Go and put your trust in him, and his answer will be—"I have loved thee with an everlasting love, therefore with loving-kindness have I drawn thee." There will be no doubt about his having chosen *you*, when you have chosen *him*.[17]

The Calvinist knows that the end goal of his election is to be made completely like Christ in his character. What an awesome thought! Jesus the first-born will have many brothers and sisters, all of whom will bear his likeness perfectly. With such a promise and vision before us, how can we Calvinists waste time making the Christian experience seem like it is focused on academic theology? Christ intends that we would be actively engaged in being "with him" so that he might make us less and less like ourselves and more and more like himself. Our Calvinism should lead us to an overpowering sense that our lives are not our own. We were chosen not to pursue our own agenda but his! We should be actively committed to "work out [our] own salvation with fear and trembling, for it is God who works in [us], both to will and to work for his good pleasure" (Philippians 2:12–13).

✳ ✳ ✳

Lord, help me not to be a theologian instead of a disciple.

Gracious Father,

I confess that too often I have contented myself with knowledge when I have not even begun to pursue holiness. I have rested arrogantly on what I know, instead of humbly acknowledging what I don't. I have overfed my intellect while letting my affections go hungry. I have found more joy in winning one of your children to my theology than to winning a lost one to Christ. It is amazing that you would have chosen one as fickle and sinful as I am, gracious God. Thank you for your unconditional election of me.

Let me now pursue the very thing for which I was chosen, to be daily invested in becoming less and less like me and more and more like your son, Jesus.

In his name, amen.

Three
BY LOVING GOD'S SOVEREIGNTY MORE THAN GOD HIMSELF

One of the least celebrated perks of being a pastor is the opportunity to meet interesting people. It's like reality TV, except in 3D and interactive.

I know of a church elder who actually called himself a widower because he considered his wife to be "spiritually dead." True story—tragic, yes, but also bizarre enough to be humorous. Infamous in many churches is the "serial courter,"[18] a young man who makes a habit of approaching young ladies in the congregation (always the attractive ones) and telling them that it's God's will for them to get married.

But my favorite is one I'll call "Jeopardy Jane." Years earlier, Jane had been the winning contestant on a TV game show, racking up a streak of victories that had gained her a pretty sizeable chunk of change. Talking with her was genuinely interesting. I remember asking several questions about Alex Trebek and how they paid her and whether there was tension with the other contestants and how she prepared. Each answer she gave was more interesting than the one before …the first time, anyway. For Jeopardy Jane was known for a stupefying predictability—every single conversation you had with her ended up veering back toward Jeopardy. After about the fourth time, it got pretty old.

I have often wondered if enthusiastic Calvinists come across this way, even to other Christians. Small-group Bible studies tend to be ripe opportunities for the one-track Calvinist. You know the drill. The group's facilitator asks everyone to share their observations on a particular verse or concept—say, the topic of prayer. Each member unfolds an insight while the Calvinist starts salivating at the chance to throw a little reformation spice into the mix. Cheerful Chuck opines on the joy of knowing that God hears and cares about all of his requests. Sweet Sarah talks about how precious her time is with her heavenly Father each morning before her day gets really busy. Then Reformed Ralph offers this valid remark, "Had God never taken the initiative to regenerate my dead heart and mind, I couldn't even pray." The group nods in agreement (except for the visitor who doesn't know what *regenerate* means) and thanks Ralph for his insight.

Let's say this is one of the first times that Ralph has spoken in the group. His comment is fresh and thought provoking; it's certainly not something the others have normally pondered when they think about prayer.

Now imagine Ralph comes consistently for months as a regular part of the group. The discussion topics vary from A (assurance of salvation) to Z (zeal for evangelism) and Reformed Ralph has a response to every one. When they talk about repentance, Ralph notes that no man can do this unless God first grants repentance. The night abortion is discussed, Ralph waxes eloquent on some of the internal debates among Calvinists regarding the election and/or reprobation of infants. Even the night Sweet Sarah talks about teaching teenage girls' modesty, Ralph says that these young ladies need to be reminded that "they are God's chosen ones" and suggests that must have something to do with skirt length. Eventually people start drifting whenever Ralph opens his mouth. He's so predictable; the Calvinistic equivalent of Jeopardy Jane.

Going Cage-Stage

It would be a mistake to one-dimensionalize Reformed Ralph. People are complicated and usually have an intricate web of reasons driving what they think and do. Ralph may be a devoted husband, father, boss, employee, son, and neighbor. Nevertheless, something has happened deep within him that makes him relish Calvinism and share that enthusiasm every chance he gets. Many seasoned Reformed thinkers refer to Ralph and his ilk as "Cage-Stage Calvinists."[19] That is, overly zealous Calvinists who perhaps ought to caged up for a while so they can't do any harm.

It's a level of enthusiasm similar to that of the tech

geeks who trumpet the superiority of their favorite gadget or operating system. Mac or PC? Android or iPhone? Hard-core fan blogs can depict alternative approaches to computing the way Stephen King describes hellish creatures from some parallel dimension. This kind of banter can be fun, and occasionally helpful to the consumer. More often than not, though, zealotry untempered by wisdom is just obnoxious and obsessive—whether your passion is computing or theology.

Without trying to go too deeply into the psychology of being in Cage Stage, it seems to me there are at least three reasons we wind up there: joy, pride, and anger.

<u>Joy.</u> For me, the discovery of God's sovereignty was deeply related to the joy of my conversion. Growing up in a loving but thoroughly agnostic household where I was truly the dumbest one of the pack, I finally understood that the only reason I became a Christian was that God had unconditionally elected me from eternity past to be his child. My somewhat baffling conversion story now made glorious sense! Yet I would be lying through my teeth if I told you that was the *only* reason I talked about election and predestination all the time.

<u>Pride.</u> I soon discovered that Calvinism was what one of my buddies calls "a thinking man's theology."[20] To be a solid and thoroughgoing Calvinist, you have to *think*—to be academically and systematically rigorous in your study of the Bible. For me, there was a good deal of ego-stroking pride in showing my less enlightened friends all the awesome things I had grasped in Scripture; God, forgive me for this arrogance.

Anger. Some Reformed people feel flat-out betrayed by former churches, pastors, and sometimes even their own parents. John Piper has diagnosed this anger-induced behavior within the Calvinist ranks:

> When a person comes to see the doctrines of grace in the Bible, he is often amazed that he missed it, and he can sometimes become angry. He can become angry that he grew up in a church or home where they never talked about what is really there in Romans 8, 1 Corinthians 2, and Ephesians 2. They never talked about it—they skipped it—and he is angry that he was misled for so long.[21]

Anger is a powerful force that can often add a dash of imagined righteous indignation to a prophet-like quest that aims to undo the harmful effects of Arminian thought. An Arminian friend actually asked me once, "Is it just me, or are some of you guys more passionate about Arminians becoming Calvinists than you are about unbelievers becoming believers?" It stung because it's true. So while I cannot prove with any empirical precision that anger is at the heart of much "in-your-face" Calvinism, I think Piper might be on to something.

Having said all that, my goal in this chapter is not to psychoanalyze cage-stagers—the heart is something only the Lord can ultimately see clearly. Instead, I want to spotlight a danger to which all Calvinists, not just cage-stagers, can be prone: loving God's sovereignty more than God himself.

God Has More Than One Attribute

It is common to hear a Reformed person say; "I see God's sovereignty on every page of the Bible." Who could argue with this? I remember the liberating experience of no longer fearing passages I once sought to ignore or explain away. Acts 13:48 used to tie me up in knots: "And when the Gentiles heard this, they began rejoicing and glorifying the word of the Lord, and *as many as were appointed to eternal life believed*." Finally, I didn't need an elaborate claim that Luke was simply emphasizing the inclusion of the Gentiles into the new people of God. Or that this passage assumes God's foreknowledge of the choice the listeners made as the *basis* of God appointing them to eternal life. I could simply accept what it said—before the foundation of the world, God chose some unworthy sinners (like me!) to become his children. Period!

Seeing this truth in Scripture is a stunning, glorious illumination. It comes as a huge relief to realize that God is utterly sovereign and that the Bible is actually saturated with this truth. The problem comes when we isolate particular passages or the concept of sovereignty itself as the headings under which everything else in Scripture is subordinated—one of the fundamental mistakes in Bible interpretation. The Puritans would rise up and slap us silly.

> Again, the glory of one attribute is more seen in one work than in another: in some things there is more of his goodness, in other things more of his wisdom is

seen, and in others more of his power. But in the work of redemption *all his perfections and excellencies* shine forth in their greatest glory.[22]

Of all people, Calvinists should be known for talking about "all his perfections and excellencies." All!

Did God sovereignly open up our hearts so we could go out into all the world and talk exclusively about what opened up our hearts? Or did he regenerate our lifeless souls in order that we would proclaim the *excellencies* (plural!) of him who called us out of darkness into his marvelous light (see 1 Peter 2:9)? Some Calvinists seem to think we were saved to proclaim God's sovereignty rather than God *himself*.

Imagine a man who has been blind his whole life. He has a wonderful wife and lovely children whom he has never actually seen. He lives each day in a world flooded with light and color, things he cannot begin to imagine despite the best efforts of his family and friends to describe and explain.

One day a team of ocular surgeons, brain specialists, and engineers from Google's Neuron Division come up with an amazing new instrument—the Sight-O-Matic 6000 (a.k.a. Google See). Thanks to this technological miracle, the man's sight is fully restored. In a short time, he goes from complete blindness to perfect 20/20 vision.

Naturally, he begins to make talk-show appearances. He writes a book, starts a blog and a Facebook fan page, and Hollywood comes knocking, offering to make a movie based on his life; they think they can get Matt Damon.

How odd would it be if the book, the blog, the Facebook page, the talk-show appearances, and the movie all focused on the Sight-O-Matic 6000? Would it not seem strange if there were few references to his wife's beauty, his kid's sparkling eyes, his appreciation of color, or his fascination with nature? Sure, the Sight-O-Matic 6000 is seriously cool, and no one can argue that it led to his astonishing life-change. But was the purpose of this amazing device to make the patient obsessed with the device itself?

The sovereignty of God is truly awesome in its power to put new life into the sinner's soul. But God saved us to "see and savor" much more than just his sovereignty.[23] While relishing the sovereignty of God in salvation is good and healthy,[24] relishing *only* God's sovereignty is unhealthy and lopsided.

The one-track Calvinist fixated on God's sovereignty as expressed through predestination is in the dangerous position of elevating one of God's attributes over all others — each attribute unique and unparalleled in its perfection and infinitude. He may zone out through a sermon until the exhilarating moment when the preacher shares a quote from Calvin, Edwards, or Spurgeon. She may half-heartedly lip-sync a song celebrating God's love and mercy, only to light up when she sees the Sovereign Grace copyright at the bottom of the slide ("Okay, now I know what they mean by the 'love' and 'mercy' of God!") He may drop a little T.U.L.I.P. petal into the conversation at every possible opportunity in his small group.

This world desperately needs to see a robust, healthy Calvinism that celebrates the fullness of God's ways and works—not a lopsided Christian who cannot get off of the hobbyhorse of God's sovereignty.

Letting Calvinism Do Its Wonderful Work

There is hope for the one-track Calvinist, however, if he simply allows the Reformed faith to affect him as it should. Knowing that God chose to open our eyes begs the simple question: what does he want us to see? Isn't it interesting that most Christians are not instant Calvinists the moment they come to faith in Christ? In my own case it took several years of reading, interacting with Scripture, talking with others, and listening to sermons before I realized that God had done all the work in my salvation, even granting me the gift of repentance and the faith to believe. Much like the anonymous hymn writer taught,

> I sought the Lord, and afterward I knew
> He moved my soul to seek him, seeking me;
> It was not I that found, O Saviour true,
> No, I was found of thee.[25]

It really was an amazing discovery to realize that God had done all the work to bring me to Christ. Yet the window of time between my new birth and my discovery of Reformed theology was anything but meaningless. I learned wonderful things in those years: how to pray, how to share my faith with others, how to write and deliver my own testimony, the value of Christian fellowship in general and the local church in particular. I learned what it meant to worship, fast, read and memorize and meditate on Scripture, repent, forgive, and reconcile. I enjoyed a host of experiences that all stoked my love for and devotion to Christ.

God was most definitely at work in my life at that time, and here's the thing—I wasn't even a Calvinist! God had wonderfully saved me in his sovereign, electing grace, but apparently Calvinism was not the first thing he wanted me to grasp. Despite my immature theology, God gave me many rich truths to see and savor with my spiritually revived eyes. Now, as a Calvinist, none of those other truths have disappeared. I can simply now better appreciate the precious sovereignty of God in ordaining a life for me, sweetened by so many graces … and so many of his multiple excellencies!

The puritan John Owen was perhaps the most learned Calvinist ever to walk the earth (except maybe for the guy this theological system was named after), but he was also a man who knew how to let his doctrine affect him. May his words of advice help us be well-grounded, well-balanced Calvinists:

> If we regularly beheld the glory of Christ our Christian walk with God would become more sweet and pleasant, our spiritual light and strength would grow daily stronger and our lives would more gloriously represent the glory of Christ. Death itself would be most welcome to us.[26]

✻ ✻ ✻

Lord, help me not to love a doctrine about you more than I love you.

Sovereign God,

Eternity will not be sufficient time for expressing the gratitude you are owed. I was a sinner, a rebel, and a traitor. I love darkness and hated your light and never would have embraced your Son unless you had first chosen me in eternity past, then sent Jesus to die for my sins, and finally sent your Spirit to breathe life into my dead, rotten heart. Why would you have done such a thing for me, dear Lord, when I deserve nothing but judgment? I can only answer with your words—for the praise of your glory and grace.

Thank you for allowing me to see you in all of your marvelous excellencies. Help me learn more of you each and every day. May my belief in your sovereignty never eclipse my wonder and adoration for all of your attributes.

Amen.

Four
BY LOSING AN URGENCY IN EVANGELISM

Burger King is not the kind of place top-secret information is usually spilled. Subterranean rooms in the Pentagon, sure. Maybe the dim back alleys of old, decrepit cities. But a fast food joint? Nevertheless, several years ago a friend of mine dropped a bomb on me not five feet from a 6-year-old boy's birthday party. It was borderline chaos as the children overran that restaurant—they were a rampaging horde of short people in cardboard crowns. I could hardly hear over the joyful din, but when my friend leaned across the booth to share his secret with me, it felt like he and I were the only two people in the world.

About a month earlier, his non-Christian mother had succumbed to breast cancer, and in the months leading up to her death I had been urging my friend to share the gospel with her. It was a hard situation. This woman had never been particularly kind or communicative, and in a "Cat's in the Cradle" kind of way, her adult son had virtually no relationship with the woman who had brought him into the world. Leaning across the remnants of our Value Meals, my friend said matter-of-factly,

"Greg, I never talked with her about the gospel. And I know this is a 'Calvinist violation,' but we both know that it *doesn't matter*. If she wasn't chosen, she wasn't chosen. Case closed."

The Secret Is Out?

My friend is a committed Christian. He is well read. He is a staunch Calvinist. And in his mind he had just "outed" what he considered a mutually shared "secret" that all Calvinists know but dare not admit for obvious PR reasons: evangelism is not really a big deal. The guy who starts every day tiptoeing through the T.U.L.I.P.s on his way to a preordained day at the office? Sure, he has to *say* that evangelism is important—the means of the elect coming to faith, the great cause of the church in the world, blah, blah, blah—yet at the end of the day, it really doesn't matter.

Or does it?

Many aspects of my friend's rationale for not sharing the gospel with his dying mother are heartbreakingly tragic. Nearly as tragic is the black eye this kind of attitude gives the Reformed cause. Think about it for a minute. What is almost always the first response of our non-Calvinist friends after hearing our five-point presentations?

- "Well, then, what's the point of evangelism?"
- "Why pray?"

- "I guess we can just sit on our behinds and let the 'elect' come to faith all by themselves."

Even the great John Wesley mocked the Calvinism of his dear friend Whitefield in one of his sermons:

> One might say to our adversary, the devil, "Thou fool, why dost thou roar about any longer? Thy lying in wait for souls is as needless and useless as our preaching. Hearest thou not, that God hath taken thy work out of thy hands; and that he doeth it much more effectually? Thou, with all thy principalities and powers, canst only so assault that we may resist thee; but he can irresistibly destroy both body and soul in hell! Thou canst only entice; but his unchangeable decrees, to leave thousands of souls in death, compels them to continue in sin, till they drop into everlasting burnings. Thou temptest; he forceth us to be damned; for we cannot resist his will. Thou fool, why goest thou about any longer, seeking whom thou mayest devour?"[27]

So Wesley sarcastically "told the devil" to stop with his pesky demonic resistance to the spread of the gospel. I can't imagine what Wesley would have said had he been sitting in my Burger King booth barely three centuries later! Certainly it would have been one more piece of "evidence" of the catastrophic effects of Reformed theology on evangelism.

Now, hear me out on this: Wesley's comments are unfair and based upon an absurd caricature of Calvinism. But before we get too tough on him, let's remind ourselves that this founder of Methodism was no lightweight when it came to reaching out to the lost. He practiced what he preached. Many historians estimate that he traveled (often by horseback) more than 200,000 miles and preached more than 40,000 sermons in his lifetime.[28] With such an evangelistic life he earned some street cred that should give us pause to think and consider how we Calvinists handle evangelism. If my friend was truly sharing an "insider's secret" that day in the restaurant, then Calvinism has a huge problem. In fact, if that "secret" is fair and accurate, I would be among the first to argue that Calvinism has been completely discredited as a theology and all its adherents ought to abandon it immediately.

Thankfully, however, it's not even close to fair or accurate. Even a cursory reading of church history reveals men like Edwards, Brainerd, Spurgeon, Carey and, in a stroke of wonderfully providential irony, George Whitefield (Wesley's dear friend), as just a few of many stellar examples of soul-winning Calvinists. So let's be clear. My Burger King friend was *not* spilling the beans about something the Reformed community has spent years trying to cover up. But I didn't tell you this story merely to dismiss his comments. I'm convinced he was onto something. I believe he unknowingly revealed a truth far more subtle, but nearly as damaging to the Reformed cause.

It's this: a temptation to use our Calvinism as an excuse for lessening our urgency in reaching the lost.

It's Our Turn to Commend Calvinism

If you have been a Calvinist for more than a few weeks, you have probably heard about the stellar evangelists I mentioned above. Most Reformed people learn of the many Calvinists in church history who have boldly preached the gospel and reached the lost. If somebody erroneously says, "Calvinists don't care about the unreached," we are poised to extol the evangelistic efforts of Whitefield or Spurgeon.

But hold on a minute. That's our "proof" that Calvinists are evangelistic? Stuff that happened *hundreds of years ago*?

If we modern-day Calvinists were known for our zeal in sharing the gospel with the lost, we would not even need to mention these heroes of history. More importantly, the detractors of Calvinism would not even raise the issue. As people see how we relate to the unsaved—with such love and generosity—they should be *surprised* to learn that we believe in unconditional election and limited atonement.

I would love to tell you that since becoming a Calvinist, I have surprised people that way on a regular basis. I do remember a few times when fellow Calvinists and I encouraged each other to evangelize lost people knowing that God's sovereign power to save should embolden our efforts. I carried a unique joy into those particular evangelistic encounters, thinking, "God may have elected this person, and I may be the chosen means of introducing him to Christ." Sadly though, such experiences have been rare. More often I have unpacked T.U.L.I.P. on a fast-food napkin to impress my Christian friends. Or I have taken out my "silver bullet" verses (yes, that's what I actually called them) to "put this deranged Arminian out of his misery" (yes, that's what I actually said).[29]

Alas, I cannot say that many people have been surprised to learn I am a Calvinist. And while it may feel great to point to Reformed people who were evangelistic centuries ago, Whitefield is no longer here to commend a healthy, robust, evangelistic Calvinism.

It's our turn to do it. You and me.

In a great little article, "How to Teach and Preach Calvinism,"[30] John Piper offers ten tips. While they are all excellent, points 4 and 5 stand out:

> 4. Make Spurgeon and Whitefield your models rather than Owen or Calvin, because the former were evangelists and won many people to Christ in a way that is nearer to our own day.

> 5. Be an evangelist and a missions mobilizer so that the criticism that Calvinism dulls a passion for the lost is put to silence.

Notice the exhortation is not to *quote* Spurgeon or Whitefield but to *make* them our models. Too often we hide behind our historical big brothers rather than follow them down the very path they worked to carve out for us.

How exactly do we follow them? Were these men "special" somehow, made from better stuff than us? Interestingly, they were not even Bible characters. If we can let James remind us that "Elijah was a man with a nature like ours, and he prayed fervently that it might not rain, and for three years and six months it did not rain on the earth" (James 5:17), then we can certainly be confident that Spurgeon, Whitefield, and Carey were men just like us. They were not special; they simply let their Calvinism shape them—as it should still shape us!

It's Our Turn to Imitate Paul

While it may be an inside joke among Reformed folks that the apostle Paul was a Calvinist, who can argue it's not true? In Romans 9 alone (and Ephesians 1; Romans 8, 10, and 11; Galatians 1; and 2 Thessalonians 1) he makes it abundantly clear that salvation comes solely and exclusively through God's unconditional election of particular sinners before the foundation of the world. In addition, the apostle undoubtedly took great *personal* comfort from this truth:

> Paul, a servant of Christ Jesus, called to be an apostle, *set apart for the gospel of God* (Romans 1:1).

> But when he who had *set me apart before I was born*, and who called me by his grace (Galatians 1:15).

> Paul, an apostle of Christ Jesus *by the will of God* according to the promise of the life that is in Christ Jesus (2 Timothy 1:1).

But Paul's delight in God's rich mercy in his own election did not make him rest on his laurels. On the contrary, it made him realize another aspect of God's sovereignty in salvation: evangelism. Paul suffered for the sake of evangelism because he was convinced that sending the elect out *as evangelists* is as much a part of God's heart as is *saving the elect*.

It's hard to imagine many 21st-century Christians (especially us in the West) embracing what Paul was willing to experience for the sake of the gospel (see 2 Corinthians 11:23-28 and Philippians 1:15-17). But consider this: would we respect Paul any less if a few of the tiny, obscure cities mentioned in Acts where he preached (often at his own peril) had been missing from his itinerary? What if the Bible were written a little differently, recording only half as many cities receiving visits from Paul? Paul would still be Paul, the preeminent church planter and evangelist among early Christians. He could have avoided or at least minimized his severe trials by one simple concession: taking his foot off the missionary pedal!

Paul never *had* to engage in any of the evangelistic activities that brought him such hardship. Yet he kept going. Why? Many answers could be supplied: the glory of God, the joy of seeing sinners converted, the overriding passion of his life's purpose. Certainly we could find passages to support all of these motivations. One motivation, however, is too often overlooked.

Paul knew there were elect sinners waiting to be converted to Christ. He knew that his sovereign God had a massive number of people chosen before time to be adopted into the family of the redeemed. And he wanted to see it happen.

This "Calvinism" motivated Paul. Even more than motivating him to share the gospel, it helped him endure immense trials because of the gospel. Here was the leading author of the New Testament and a man who arguably had more insight into the character and ways of God than you or I ever will, and if we need proof that he could believe 100 percent in predestination *and* 100 percent in evangelism, here it is: "I *endure everything* for the *sake of the elect*, that *they also may obtain the salvation* that is in Christ Jesus with eternal glory" (2 Timothy 2:10). Paul paid a high personal price, suffering hardship and spending himself to bring the gospel and preach the gospel to people *who were already certain to be saved*! Why?

Because the saved are the means God uses to reach the lost.

Any temptation to feel that the doctrine of election frees us from the need to evangelize results from a false view of Calvinism. It certainly wasn't Paul's view! Are we going to let a misreading of John Calvin's human arguments made more than 1400 years after the last letter of the New Testament was penned so alter our reading of infallible Scripture that our practice of evangelism is fundamentally opposed to that of the apostles and direct disciples of Jesus?

What a powerful, practical concept—there are elect people out there. Some have been spiritually reborn, but many are still *waiting* to be spiritually reborn. Yet because the latter group is elect, we have a guarantee: there will always be sinners who respond to the free offer of the gospel and obtain the salvation they have been chosen to receive! How do we know they are still out there? Because Christ has not yet returned, which means that the work—which includes *our* work—is not yet complete.

The Bible is clear:

- We *know* that God is sovereign.
- We *know* that he has elected people to be saved.
- We *know* that he is at work in the earth toward that certain goal.
- And we *know* that he wants to use us to help make it happen.

I cannot make it any clearer than that. It certainly does not need to be more complicated.

A good friend of mine talks about "Reformed giddi-ness." He describes it as that wonderful feeling when you know good news about someone's fortunes before they know. It would be somewhat like having the honor of presenting someone with a large cash prize and relishing the moments before you put it in her hands. She doesn't know what's coming, but you sure do! Granted, we do not know the individual identities of the elect, but we do know that whenever the gospel is going forth, there are chosen people waiting to receive a shocking gift—the greatest possible gift. This truth enables us to love and serve all people genuinely, while we wait on God to reveal his special, sovereign love to his own.

> The non-elect in this world are faceless men as far as we are concerned. We know that they exist, but we do not and cannot know who they are, and it is as futile as it is impious for us to try and guess …Our calling as Christians is not to love God's elect, and them only, but to love our neighbour, irrespective of whether he is elect or not.[31]

* * *

Lord, let your sovereignty compel me to speak of you.

Seeking Savior,

Not one soul would ever choose you unless you chose him first. While it breaks my heart to confess it, I know that I never would have run to you had you simply waited for me. Even though you are the only worthy choice of every man who has ever lived, sin has so wrecked us that we are incapable of ever choosing you. Thank you for sovereign grace. Thank you for your gracious, undeserved election. For predestining us to be adopted as sons.

Now, Lord, give me a burning passion to endure all things for the sake of the elect, that they too may receive the same mercy that I have received. Would you convict me every time I pervert your sovereignty into an excuse for my own sloth and self-indulgence. Please break my heart, Lord, for the lost, knowing that I every time I live and speak among unbelievers, I might expect to be wonderfully surprised by a sinner who cries out, "Save me, Lord Jesus!"

Amen.

Five
BY LEARNING ONLY FROM OTHER CALVINISTS

A few years ago, driving around an unfamiliar city, I was scanning the AM radio dial for some sports talk when I unexpectedly found myself riveted by an interview with a well-known Christian leader. "Who is this guy?" I asked myself. "He sure sounds familiar." He was warm, thoughtful, and balanced. The interviewer was asking this pastor for his take on the importance of the local church, and it went something like this:

"You've been a pastor for over 30 years now?"

"That's right. It's been quite a journey."

"Would you say that you love the local church?"

He chuckled. "It has some trying times, no doubt, but I would say without hesitation, 'Yes!' with all of my heart!"

"What would you say is your number-one takeaway insight regarding the church after all these years?"

He did not hesitate: "There is nothing better than the local church when the local church is working right."

I love the local church. I have read countless books and listened to innumerable sermons on this theme, but I have never read or heard a better stand-alone sentence on the subject than, "There is nothing better than the local church when the local church is working right."

Pulling off to the shoulder of the road to listen more closely, I was soon enjoying a brilliant, impromptu seminar on the topic. The guy was just doing a great job. As the exchange wound down, I became even more curious about the identity of this mystery pastor who had such passion for and insight into the institution to which I have devoted my life. That's when the interviewer burst my bubble by thanking his special guest, Pastor Bill Hybels, for being with him time in the studio that day.

Bill Hybels? From Willow Creek Church? Huh?

I sat in the car trying to wrap my head around what had just happened. I loved what Hybels had said (and have since learned that the sentence that caught my attention is essentially a mission statement for Bill Hybels and the international side of the Willow Creek Association[32]) and thought it was well worth passing on to others. Yet this particular pastor was perhaps the best-known advocate of the "seeker-sensitive" model of doing church, which most Reformed thinkers and pastors dislike. And he's certainly no Calvinist!

That's when I actually found myself saying, "Man, I wish Tim Keller had said all of that!"[33]

More Than a Broken Clock

When I returned home from this trip I conducted a series of brief experiments on some of my Reformed friends. I would share the quotation, without attribution, and ask them what they thought of it. Most considered it a good, pithy sentence with a lot of potential to unpack and apply for the good of the church. Then I would note the source of the quotation and watch my friends almost visibly squirm, just like I had. Suddenly, it seemed less biblical, too surfacey, not deep enough for sanctioned use. What was going on here?

Upon learning the source of the comment, most of my trial audience invoked some variation on the phrase, "Even a broken clock is right twice a day." Suddenly we wanted to dismiss Hybels' wisdom as little more than common sense—maybe even good luck (yes, we actually speculated that perhaps he had stumbled into saying something biblically accurate by random chance).

Is this healthy? Do we Reformed folks tend to assume that, because we are right on predestination, we are the only ones who can actually be right on *everything else*? Or can we allow the possibility that God has given genuine wisdom and insight to other kinds of believers from whom we can benefit? Even if they are not Calvinists?

Some of my friends say, "Hybels has significantly minimized the centrality of the Bible and theology in his approach to doing church, so I don't really care what he has to say about anything?"[34] I can certainly understand that reaction. But we must be extremely cautious. Scripture is calling us Calvinists (along with all believers) to be inten-

tionally charitable in our assessment of others' ministries
and motives. Consider the following clear admonitions:

> Do not speak evil against one another, brothers.
> The one who speaks against a brother or judges his
> brother, speaks evil against the law and judges the law.
> (James 4:11)

> Why do you pass judgment on your brother? Or you,
> why do you despise your brother? For we will all stand
> before the judgment seat of God. (Romans 14:10)

> Therefore do not pronounce judgment before the
> time, before the Lord comes, who will bring to light
> the things now hidden in darkness and will disclose
> the purposes of the heart. Then each one will receive
> his commendation from God. (1 Corinthians 4:5)

Categorizing brothers and sisters in Christ is almost
second nature. I do it myself. But we must encourage
each other to make charitable judgments about those
who claim Christ as Savior. I love the way Ken Sande
puts it:

> Making a charitable judgment means that out of
> love for God you strive to believe the best about
> others until you have facts to prove otherwise. In
> other words, if you can reasonably interpret what
> someone has said or done in two possible ways, God
> calls you to embrace the positive interpretation

over the negative, or at least to postpone making any judgment at all until you can acquire conclusive facts.[35]

I think the best and most charitable judgment I could draw from my experience listening to Hybels is that God graciously allowed me to learn something wonderful from a man outside of my own theological camp. And I am convinced that this should not be a rare occurrence. Our non-Reformed brother and sisters in Christ are not like broken clocks that are only ever right once in a great while, nor simply by accident.

The Curious Case of Lewis

C. S. Lewis is considered one of the most respected spokesmen for Christianity, even among Calvinists.[36] Looking back over my sermon manuscripts, I see that I quoted him eleven times in just the past year! But whenever I mention him from the pulpit, I will typically say something like, "Now remember, in terms of theology, when Lewis is hot he's really hot! But when he's bad …well, he's abysmal."

In light of Lewis' less-than-orthodox convictions regarding key doctrines, J. I. Packer pondered the perplexing love affair Christians (including Packer himself) have with the Oxford scholar.

He did not attend an evangelical place of worship nor fraternize with evangelical organizations …. By ordinary evangelical standards, his idea about the Atonement (archetypal penitence, rather than penal substitution), and his failure ever to mention justification by faith when speaking of the forgiveness of sins, and his apparent hospitality to baptismal regeneration, and his noninerrantist view of biblical inspiration, plus his quiet affirmation of purgatory and of the possible final salvation of some who have left this world as nonbelievers, were weaknesses; they led the late, great Martyn Lloyd-Jones, for whom evangelical orthodoxy was mandatory, to doubt whether Lewis was a Christian at all.[37]

Let's be honest: C. S. Lewis had, at best, an elusive relationship with evangelical Christianity, never mind Calvinism! Yet many (including me) find enough good in his writings to commend him to others. Isn't this proof enough that we instinctively know we can learn from people in other theological traditions? I would argue that non-Calvinists like Philip Yancey, Bill Hybels, Rick Warren, and Greg Laurie have far fewer differences with us than Lewis had. However, for some reason, there is often a strong reluctance among Calvinists to even consider learning from such thinkers.

I am not suggesting that Calvinists should feel guilty about feeding on a steady diet of Reformed thinkers and teachers. I, for one, am not about to replace my three favorite podcast preachers (Piper, Driscoll, and MacArthur) with Arminian preachers just so I can be "evangelically correct" and tell others how "balanced" I am. But I do think it may help us to go outside of our own theological camp occasionally and see what some other people are saying. We simply need to be careful about a "non-Calvinists need not apply" mentality when thinking broadly about the body of Christ.

Earlier, I mentioned the conflict between Whitefield and Wesley in 18th-century England over the subject of election. Both men had preached the gospel outdoors to tens of thousands of people, something radically unconventional at that time. At the start of their ministries they agreed not to let their differences divide them in preaching the gospel to unbelievers. Needless to say, Whitefield was deeply hurt when his Arminian friend railed on Calvinism in a published sermon. Reluctantly, Whitefield finally responded in writing himself. Even though he passionately opposed Wesley's position (and successfully dismantled it, in my opinion), he ends his letter with these words.

> Dear Sir, these things ought not so to be. God knows my heart, as I told you before, so I declare again, nothing but a single regard to the honour of Christ has forced this letter from me. I love and honour you for his sake; and when I come to judgment, will thank you before men and angels, for what you have, under God, done for my soul.[38]

Whitefield the Calvinist expected to *thank* his Arminian friend on the Day of Judgment for all that Wesley had done for his soul. Apparently, Whitefield did not feel that his friend was merely a broken clock who inadvertently got a couple of things right on rare occasions. Whitefield genuinely loved Wesley and learned from him.

Thankful for Every Providence

I believe that if I do not pause and thank God for *all* of the people he has brought into my life, I am killing Calvinism in the worst way. God has so ordained and orchestrated my life, down to the finest detail, that to refuse to see God's hand in bringing many wonderful non-Calvinists into my life would be a rejection of Reformed theology.

So here we go.

I am thankful for a middle-school speech therapist, Mrs. Sadem, (whom I've never been able to track down), for going out on a limb and violating every public-school policy on the books in order to tell me that Jesus died for my sins. As far as I know, she was the first seed-planter God sent my way. She was no more than 4-feet 10-inches tall and belonged to a Full Gospel Tabernacle church (so, not a Calvinist—not even close). She did not lead me to Christ, but I never forgot her joy in Jesus, nor my attraction to that joy, which was totally foreign to me.

I'm thankful for the pre-Calvinist version of Matt Smith. We became best friends (still are) at 14, and he faithfully preached the essential truths of the gospel to me. I remember him saying, "Greg, there's two things I know. Number 1: You have to be born again to go to heaven. Number 2: You're not born again." Theologically he was a mess—a mullet-wearing, television-evangelist-quoting firebrand. But he genuinely loved me and, by God's grace, led me to Christ. Today Matt is a Sovereign Grace pastor—thoroughly Reformed—who lives not ten minutes from me. We preach at each other's churches and pray for each other's ministries. And we often celebrate the goodness of God in those early years when Calvinism was still as foreign to us as a game of cricket is to a Texas rodeo clown.

I am thankful for the late pastor Leonard Blight, a Christian Missionary Alliance minister who loved A. W. Tozer but passionately rejected Calvinism. He was an old-school preacher who would stomp his foot and get excited about the "premillenial, pre-tribulational rapture of the church mentioned 318 times in the New Testament!" I've come to believe that there's no such thing and that it's mentioned exactly zero times,[39] but I deeply appreciate his unquestioned passion for the gospel and its saving power. He taught me that there should be a sense of urgency in the Christian life, since we are all standing on the brink of eternity. I eagerly look forward to seeing him on the other side one day.

I am thankful for Dave Shive, the finest pastor I have ever known. He has been a mentor to me in some of the darkest hours of my life. My wife, Lisa, loves him too and often asks me, "What do you think Dave would do in this situation?" He is an Old Testament scholar, and I keep urging him to write a book on the life of David, because I simply have never heard better teaching on the subject anywhere from anyone. We have spent many a breakfast wrangling over the finer points of Calvinism, and he will happily tell you or anybody else that he outright rejects Reformed theology. Of course, we each think the other is completely wrong, but to say that I have not learned anything from Dave would be a denial of the sweet providence of God in my life.

I could go on for quite some time naming others and thanking God for them, but I will resist the urge.

What about you? Have you fellowshiped with any non-Reformed folks lately? Have you tragically ruled out the possibility that God could teach you something precious through an Arminian? Can you look back on your own journey with Christ and see where he taught you through people you might now distance yourself from?

May God keep us Calvinists humble and willing to learn from anyone his providence may put in our path.

❊ ❊ ❊

Lord, help me see your hand of providence.

Precious Father,

When I think of the people you have brought into my life, I am overwhelmed with joy and gratitude. I specifically thank you for those who do not agree with me on the extent of your sovereignty in salvation. Who am I to scorn those for whom you have sent your one and only Son to suffer and die?

Teach me all that you want me to learn, Lord, from anyone, in any place, at any time. Forgive me for my pride in limiting what you may want to teach and show me. Keep my heart soft. Whatever I can learn of you is good and healing to my soul. Any anything that glorifies your name, Lord, please let me have the joy of learning it. For Jesus' sake.

Amen

Six
BY TIDYING UP THE BIBLE'S "LOOSE ENDS"

"Okay, guys let me draw a circle here on the whiteboard to illustrate this. Now pay close attention because I'm going to try and make a perfect circle without a compass."

I step up to the board and draw a huge circle and (because I've been doing this for a number of years) it is actually pretty close to perfect. I start at about 1 o'clock on the clock face, swoop my arm around in a big smooth arc, and then start to slow down as the line comes back around to the top. As I turn my back to the whiteboard and take a couple of steps toward the class full of teenage students, I can see the confusion and frustration on some of their faces. And I know exactly why.

I didn't quite close the otherwise perfect circle. There is still a small but obvious gap at the top.

Without saying anything, I then return to the whiteboard and write a series of words that include lots of "t's"

and lower case "i's"—but I don't cross any of the "t's" or
dot any of the "i's." At that point, you can almost see the
smoke coming out of the ears of some of the students.

This has been my practice in teaching the occasional
Bible course in my kids' Christian school. I like to find
out which students want closure and how frustrated they
become when they don't get it. Unclosed circles and half-
finished letters have a way of driving certain people crazy.
On one occasion, a fifteen-year-old girl raised her hand
and asked, "Mr. Dutcher. I know that you are just trying
to be funny and make a point. But could you *please* close
that circle or I think I'm going to come out of my skin?" I
put her out of her misery and closed the circle.

Sometimes Calvinists do this, too.

Closing the Circle

Like any theology, Calvinism is a *system* of doctrine. All
systems have structure, unity and, of course, closure. I
have made several references to T.U.L.I.P. in this book,
and that acrostic is really a kind of system itself. It pulls
together many strands and sections of biblical teaching
and presents them in an orderly and logical fashion.[40] If
someone asks the Calvinist, "What is your understanding
of how God saves sinners?" then he can respond with a
clear, linear answer. Having such systems is helpful. We
need good and clear categories of thinking, especially
when thinking about God. People who have questions
need solid answers with substance and will usually be put
off if we freewheel through the Bible, making reference to
seemingly random stories and passages.

Another way to say it is that systems are just convenient ways to talk in a sort of "Bible shorthand." We acknowledge that a theological system (Calvinism, or any "ism" for that matter) is really just a summary of the Bible's teaching. Yet a *summary* of Bible teaching is not to be confused with *the Bible itself*! A theology should flow from the Bible and organize various truths the Bible teaches into a set of logical propositions. But every theological system must always stand under the Bible and be continually held in check by the Bible.[41]

Several years ago, although I was pleased with being a card-carrying Calvinist, I did not fully understand that Jesus' redemptive work involved more than just *dying* for sinners. I had yet to really see that he also needed to *provide a perfect righteousness* for sinners, the righteousness that he lived out daily for 33 years on this earth.[42] Until I understood this truth more fully, I had a theology, for sure, but it was a theology in need of tweaking. Our theology should become more nuanced and rich as we let the Bible tweak and shape it. Unfortunately, some Calvinists get the order backwards, letting their theology determine what the Bible says or does not say.

Several years ago I was doing an informal study of Peter's epistles with some Reformed friends. It was largely a good study until we got into an obscure section in Second Peter where the apostle chillingly lays out the destiny of false teachers:

> But these, like irrational animals, creatures of instinct, *born to be caught and destroyed*, blaspheming about

matters of which they are ignorant, will also be *destroyed in their destruction*, suffering wrong as the wage for their wrongdoing. (2:12)

These are waterless springs and mists driven by a storm. *For them the gloom of utter darkness has been reserved*. (2:17)

We all agreed that these false teachers were clearly unsaved, and, more than that, they were destined for judgment. After talking about the evils of false doctrine and how much we want to help guard our churches against heresy, I asked the uncomfortable question. "Why do you think Peter describes these heretics as 'bought' by Christ?" I was referring to the first verse of chapter 2:

But false prophets also arose among the people, just as there will be false teachers among you, who will secretly bring in destructive heresies, even denying *the Master who bought them*, bringing upon themselves swift destruction.

It was interesting to gauge my friends' reactions to the question. One of them stared at the verse for a while and let his mental wheels turn. But my other friend's reaction was puzzling. He simply said, "Well, it doesn't matter because we know that Jesus died only for the elect." With that short reply he was ready to move on to other subjects. But how can anyone say that it does not matter?

I am a 5-point Calvinist through and through, but my theology does not give me a right to say "Oh, that verse doesn't matter." It was as if my friend simply saw the verse as a "loose end," and his theology was right there to tie it up in a neat little bow. Sadly, this kind of thinking makes the Bible a kind of "footnote" that simply exists to support our theological system. We become lazy in our study of God's Word because we never have to wrestle with complex passages.[43] Not liking the slightly open circle, the Calvinist sometimes pulls out his pencil and shades in the gap: "Ah …we know what Reformed theology says. No biggie to cross the T and dot the I in that passage. Why let those pesky little verses that don't quite cooperate with our pre-packaged theology get in the way?"

May we never dismiss or fail to take seriously a single word of Scripture. Study and learn and grow, but may we never dare to take it upon ourselves to help God out and close the circle on our own.

At Peace with Paradox

Another way to tidy up the Bible's loose ends is to unnecessarily qualify the passages that may seem to go against Calvinism. The motivation here appears to be rooted in not wanting others to get the wrong idea. We imagine, therefore, that it is the Calvinist's job to make sure no one misunderstands passages emphasizing man's responsibility to believe, or God's love for all of mankind, in a way that could make them reject Reformed theology.

I once heard a sermon from a gifted and passionately

Reformed preacher. His text portrayed one of the most tender pictures of Jesus found anywhere in the gospels:

> O Jerusalem, Jerusalem, the city that kills the prophets and stones those who are sent to it! How often would I have gathered your children together as a hen gathers her brood under her wings, and you would not! (Matthew 23:37)

There is so much in the passage: the history of man's rejection of God, the tragedy of unbelief, and, most of all, the fierce and tender compassion of our Savior. Having heard this brilliant preacher many times, I was eager to watch him unfold some of these truths in full rhetorical splendor! Instead, he spent nearly fifty minutes telling his listeners what this text did *not* mean.

- It did *not* mean that the citizens of Jerusalem had the power to choose Christ, since no man chooses Christ in his own power.
- It did *not* mean that Jesus failed in his mission to save these sinners, because Jesus perfectly fulfilled his Father's plan.
- It did *not* mean that Jesus was dying for them specifically on the cross, since he dies only for his elect.

All of these points are true of Calvinism. The only problem was that none of these points were found in the passage!

God does not need us to be his spin-doctors. When

we feel compelled to make sure that his sacred Word does not give the "wrong impression," we are really demonstrating a tremendous lack of confidence in the clarity and authority of Scripture. The Holy Spirit inspired the beautiful passage of Jesus weeping over the lost people of Jerusalem, and we must be faithful to present the text as it is written. We don't need to take ten minutes (or fifty) to defend the Calvinistic "other side of the coin."

Similarly, when our friends get caught up in Tebow-mania and ask us what John 3:16 is all about, we can confidently tell them that the verse means what it says. "God so loved the world," that he sent Jesus to us as the divine rescuer so that "whoever" believes in him would be saved. We can happily tell them that God loves them and is giving them an opportunity to put their hope and faith in Christ.[44]

When we refuse to let our theology dictate Scripture, we are free to live with large doses of paradox. We are not afraid of passages that emphasize the need for good works. We do not feel awkward about verses that call on everyone to make a choice and take a stand for the Lord. Instead, we are free to put all of our hope in our sovereign God while striving to follow everything he has commanded us to do and be.

Biblicists, Not Calvinists

Can you imagine the impact we Calvinists would make if others saw us first and foremost as people who are faithful to *Scripture*? When a Reformed person says, "It doesn't matter what the verse says," or "That particular passage you're looking at may appear to support free will, but it really doesn't," who could blame anyone for being suspicious about our motives? It's as if we are wearing T-shirts that say, "We Have a Theology to Protect."

Could this be one of many reasons why some Arminians are reluctant even to consider Calvinism? Is it possible we have given them the impression that we are living more by human dictates imposed upon Scripture than we are living by Scripture itself?

A far more important question: are we in fact guilty of that? Are we so wedded to a theological system that we have lost the wonder of living by God's perfect Word?

Non-Calvinists have every right to be suspicious when they see us playing fast and loose with the Bible. If we are Calvinists because we've been persuaded primarily by present-day authors and teachers, or even by reading the *Institutes*, then our friends can easily and understandably dismiss our Calvinism as a tidy philosophy dreamed up by man. But if we can show them that our convictions about God's sovereignty in salvation are rooted in a careful study of Scripture—even if we can't always close the circle perfectly!—then our friends can have confidence that they are interacting with God's truth, not man's opinion.

I close this chapter with one Calvinist esteeming another Calvinist, not for his polished theology, but for his love of God's Word. Let us learn from how touched Charles Spurgeon was by John Bunyan's complete immersion in Scripture:

Read anything of his and you will see that it is almost like reading the Bible itself. He had studied our Authorized Version, which will never be bettered, as I judge, till Christ shall come. He had read it till his very soul was saturated with Scripture and though his writings are charmingly full of poetry, yet he cannot give us his *Pilgrim's Progress*—that sweetest of all prose poems—without continually making us feel and say, "Why, this man is a living Bible!" Prick him anywhere—his blood is Bibline—the very essence of the Bible flows from him! He cannot speak without quoting a text, for his very soul is full of the Word of God.[45]

✳ ✳ ✳

Lord, I praise you for your perfect Word.

Only Wise God,
   You have given me a treasure—your very Word. I deserve to be left in the darkness, without any light or insight in this sin-soaked world. Just one sentence from you would have been a great gift, but you have given me a waterfall of truth in the pages of sacred Scripture. In it I have learned that you chose me and did everything necessary to bring me to saving faith.
   But forgive me, Lord, for using my theology as an excuse for my own laziness. Make me an unashamed workman who rightly handles your perfect Word. May others see that, by your grace, I am building my very life

upon the foundation of your truth. May this cause others to do the same.

Amen

Seven
BY BEING AN ARROGANT KNOW-IT-ALL

I just sat down to do some work on this chapter and out of sheer curiosity Googled "Calvinists." As I typed that word into the search bar, the auto-fill feature kicked in, offering me options based on the most commonly searched phrases beginning with that word. Guess what the top option was?

"Calvinists are arrogant."

Ugh.

With a certain fear and trembling, I clicked on the search phrase. The first seven or eight hits revealed an even split, about half of them agreeing and half disagreeing with the statement. The results could have been worse, but I was still a little shocked at the ready association with arrogance. Doesn't Calvinism teach humility?

Of course, Calvinists are far from monolithic in matters outside the core gospel-related categories. Ways of "doing church" and living out Reformed theology, for example, were varied even before the emergence of some of the newer manifestations of Calvinism. I'm not even sure there is such a thing as "typical" Calvinism, broadly speaking, in the 21st-century, so it would be foolish to try to generalize about "our" motivations and ways of interacting with others.

That's fine. I may not be able to speak for all of us, but I can certainly speak for myself.

As I have already noted, when I think of my own early days in the Reformed faith, I have much to be ashamed of. Only God knows how many people I hurt, confused, or just totally turned off to even considering Calvinism. I was obnoxious.

The year between college and seminary was my prime Cage Stage. Everyone would have been better off—myself included—had I been locked away for at least a few months during that time. I just could not stop scratching the itch. During this time I was so excited about the five points of Calvinism that I actually wrote a letter to a friend containing this line: "I'm concerned about you. If you will not submit to God's clear declaration about how he saves sinners, how can you ever expect to get one other thing in your life right?" Today, I look back on that statement with something like disbelief. How could I not have seen the arrogance? Who appointed me the judge of all my Christian friends? It is so obvious to me now. Back then it felt as natural and normal as telling someone not to step on a live wire. Little did I realize that I had become an arrogant know-it-all.

Why Calvinists May Struggle with Arrogance

Again, I am operating on the premise that my own struggle with Calvinistic pride has some universal application. I am, after all, a sinner like my fellow Reformers, and I suspect that others may share the same temptations and weaknesses that have characterized my own journey. Not to mention that we all share a common father in Adam, and in the case of "like father, like son," the pride that led him to defy his maker is with all of us. As Matthew Henry opined, "Grace does not run in the blood, but corruption does."[46]

Let me be clear; in no way am I suggesting that Calvinism *logically* leads to pride. On the contrary, I will end this chapter emphasizing the opposite. But our hearts can take any good thing—food, sex, money, even really good theology—and use it as an opportunity to indulge our sinful desires. Pastor Joe Thorn offers an excellent observation about this:

> When addressing the issue of "those angry Calvinists" we need to be careful and not make Calvinism the issue. It's not about Calvinism. The negativity, pride, and finger wagging is not about the Doctrines of Grace, but the heart. So, when we see such things coming from Calvinists we should seek to point out that this attitude is actually incompatible with Calvinism.[47]

I believe with all my heart that Calvinism is a treasure. It beautifully summarizes and systematizes the truths concerning our salvation revealed in Scripture. But treasure in the hands of fools is a frightening prospect, and nothing fuels a fool more than pride. I pray that my fellow Calvinists would join me in hunting down every vestige of pride in our hearts, right down to the last lingering impulse of arrogance. One of the ways we can root out pride is by understanding its causes. So let me offer two reasons I think we Calvinists often struggle with arrogance: because we love being in the know, and because we love being thought well of.

Being in the Know Is Cool

By the time we are in kindergarten, most of us have learned the delicious joy of having a secret. Recently my wife and I had to comfort our young elementary-aged son, Isaac, when he came home from school with tears in his eyes: "Timmy told Ryan a secret, and they wouldn't tell me what it was." When Isaac walked us through the sad tale, he painted Timmy and Ryan as gleefully high-fiving each other for possessing some impossibly wonderful morsel of information that Isaac was clueless about.

A shared secret—whether a trivial bit of nonsense, a shameful slab of gossip, a stock tip, or a lewd joke—is just one of several ways by which people join together to form "in" crowds. An especially powerful and enduring form of the "in" crowd involves a shared passion, like for a sports team, a method of brewing coffee, or a theological system. What they all have in common is special knowledge coupled with passion that others do not share. Combine that with the capacity for raging pride that we all have lurking in our hearts, and any kind of special knowledge can quickly lead to an attitude that says, "We get it, and you don't."

Shared passions can range from the trivial to the transcendent. On the trivial side, growing up Dutcher meant learning to love pizza, a staple in our household. Not just any old pizza would do, however. We had a core doctrine of pizza, frequently repeated by my father, so that the faith might be passed down from one generation to another: "It's not the cheese. It's not the crust. It's the *sauce*!" The unenlightened—pizza eaters who had yet to discover this fundamental truth—gave us frequent opportunity to celebrate our shared superiority. "Hey Dad, my friend Matt says Maria's Carryout is the best because of their cheese." Of course, the subtext to these comments was essentially, "What kind of imbecile would believe something so preposterous!" My father and brother and I would shake our heads in feigned sympathy.

For me, "getting" Calvinism was like a pizza secret taken to cosmological levels. It definitely provided a powerful sense of belonging to the right club. What was weird was finding out that the bulk of my Christian friends thought I had lost my mind. In time, however, I found myself enamored with the idea that I was in the "right" camp with the "right" people. A person needs to think like this for only five minutes before seeing himself as fundamentally better than his uninitiated brothers and sisters in Christ.

Of course, it's not ultimately a big deal if I'm a pizza snob or a Baltimore Ravens snob or a Starbucks snob. It's a huge deal, however, if I am a spiritual snob. What if my kids grow up thinking that non-Calvinist Christians are inferior to the Reformed? What if my congregation starts viewing itself as the *true* people of God who practice *authentic* Christianity unlike the free-will church down the road? Do I want to be responsible for helping shape a culture of pride and elitism among the Christians I'm privileged to serve?

I unhesitatingly believe in the sovereignty of God in salvation. Therefore (and this is only logical), I believe that the Arminian understanding of the sovereignty of man in salvation is wrong. But the question of application is a simple one: can I live with this theological conviction and still not look down on those with whom I disagree?

Let us start with some leading figures in the Arminian Hall of Fame. Can I say that I differ with John Wesley, C. S. Lewis, or Billy Graham on their doctrine of salvation but still see them as wonderful Christian men whom God has used mightily to advance his kingdom in this world?[48] There is something tragically ironic about a young Calvinist who may never have shared his faith with an unbeliever looking down on some of the very men who should be looked up to as gospel champions. What would you think, sports fans, of a Little League player making fun of Albert Pujols for his unconventional batting stance?

But we must not stop there. What about the count-less everyday believers who are ignorant or deeply skeptical of Calvinist doctrine? Do we honor them as well? Just because we know something that someone else has yet to see does not grant us *any* superiority. My three-year-old daughter knows things about me that my cardiologist does not, but I don't think I'll cancel my annual heart checkup anytime soon. Whenever we find ourselves overly attentive to the deficiencies in others (especially when it comes to theology), we should be very suspicious—of ourselves. Jonathan Edwards warned us of this kind of subtle arrogance:

> Spiritual pride is very apt to suspect others: whereas a humble saint is most jealous of himself, he is so suspicious of nothing in the world as he is of his own heart. The spiritually proud person is apt to find fault with other saints …and to be quick to discern and take note of their deficiencies: but the eminently humble Christian has so much to do at home, and sees so much evil in his own heart, and is so concerned about it, that he is not apt to be very busy with others' hearts.[49]

If our Calvinism has become a platform from which we look down upon others, we desperately need God's grace to convict us that this is sinful. May God let our Reformed convictions lead us first to suspect *ourselves* of pride and arrogance at every turn.

Being Thought Well of Is Even Cooler

If being in the know can tempt us to the sinful pleasure of *looking down upon others*, being thought well of can tempt us to the sinful pleasure of enjoying *being looked up to by others*. Sometimes we can be kind and gracious to non-Calvinists in an unacceptable way—on the condition that they recognize that we are awesome!

In the third chapter I made brief mention of how much I liked impressing others with my learning. Now it's time to go in to a bit more detail. Because let's face it: you can't be a Calvinist without becoming aware of some pretty impressive stuff.

In the pre-Internet stage of my early Calvinism, I was a mail-order junkie. Ligonier Ministries (R. C. Sproul) and Grace to You (John MacArthur) were my regular suppliers, and I spent every dime on my blissful new addiction. I read and listened to anything I could get my hands on and quickly learned some nifty terms and concepts:

- Imputation
- Justification
- Reprobation
- Immutable decrees
- Covenant of works
- Covenant of grace
- Federal headship of Adam and Christ
- T.U.L.I.P. and its more subtly nuanced modifications, with terms like "radical corruption" and "particular redemption"
- Passive and active righteousness

And on and on.

All of a sudden, I had more in my theological tool-box than John 3:16, WWJD, and an "emptiness inside the heart that only Jesus can fill." With all these shiny new Reformed concepts floating through my head I did what any humble follower of Christ would do: I worked hard to show off to others how much I knew!

I started a T.U.L.I.P. Bible study with my friends, who may well have attended out of fear of physical retribution. I had buckets of new knowledge to show off, and since I was too young to be a pastor who would have put an entire church through my torture sessions, my friends would have to suffice—somebody had to hear my great wisdom!

Every week I would type up—yes, on an electric typewriter—extensive notes with quotes from Berkhof, Machen, and, of course, Calvin. (Knowing that Calvin had written the *Institutes* at age 26, I thought that maybe I could do something similar at 22. Looking back on my notes, the Genevan reformer need not be concerned.) Ashamed as I am to admit it, I truly craved the compliments of the attendees. When I occasionally got one, I think I usually managed to appear self-effacing, but inside I was dancing a jig.

My "conversion" to Calvinism helped produce in me a new level of academic rigor, representing my first serious intellectual grapplings not required by an educational system. Apparently I am not alone in this; I know several people for whom Reformation thought has inspired a similar transformation. Others come to Calvinism already in possession of serious intellectual or academic credentials. John Piper offers an interesting observation on the affinity of Calvinism for "cerebral types":

> I love the doctrines of grace with all my heart, and I think they are pride-shattering, humbling, and love-producing doctrines. But I think there is an attractiveness about them to some people, in large matter, because of their intellectual rigor. They are powerfully coherent doctrines, and certain kinds of minds are drawn to that. And those kinds of minds tend to be argumentative.
>
> So the intellectual appeal of the system of Calvinism draws a certain kind of intellectual person, and that type of person doesn't tend to be the most warm, fuzzy, and tender. Therefore this type of person has a greater danger of being hostile, gruff, abrupt, insensitive, or intellectualistic.[50]

Knowledge puffs up (1 Corinthians 8:1), and without love and humility to temper our knowledge, an intellectually rigorous theology like Calvinism can be a dangerous breeding ground for pride and self-exaltation.

Here's an easy trivia game. Sometimes just revisiting passages we have read for years has a way of freshly affecting us if we let them. Look at the following verses and guess who is being described?

- "Thus, when you give to the needy, sound no trumpet before you, as the hypocrites do in the synagogues and in the streets, that *they may be praised by others*" (Matthew 6:2).

- "And they love the place of honor at feasts and the best seats in the synagogues and greetings in the marketplaces and *being called rabbi by others*" (Matthew 23:6–7).
- "For *they loved the glory that comes from man* more than the glory that comes from God" (John 12:43).

If you answered "Pharisee" then you win the prize. But look at those verses again and ask if they might be equally applicable to the proud Calvinist. I shudder as I think about the many times I enjoyed being the "theological" one in the group—the guy who knew the meaning of an obscure Old Testament passage or who could drop a little Latin or Koine Greek into a conversation. I can still remember rewinding Sproul videos to make sure I could say *posse peccare*, *posse non peccare* as smoothly as he did. Yes, the Calvinist can certainly become an arrogant know-it-all if he is not careful.

True Calvinism Cannot Lead to Pride

The irony, of course, is that Calvinism *actually lived out* can never lead to pride. The Calvinist is the one who should be clambering up to the rooftops to shout, "I am a total train wreck! I've made a mess of my life and anyone who has known me for more than five minutes can see the evidence!"

We Calvinists know with chilling clarity the corruption and evil of our own hearts. It is, then, all the more regrettable that we would ever dare think of ourselves more highly than we ought. One of my favorite Spurgeon sermons is his reflection on John 6:44, "No one can come to me unless the Father who sent me draws him." With almost scientific precision, he dismantles any notion of man as inherently good:

> We declare, upon Scriptural authority, that the human will is so desperately set on mischief, so depraved, and so inclined to everything that is evil, and so disinclined to everything that is good, that without the powerful, supernatural, irresistible influence of the Holy Spirit, no human will ever be constrained towards Christ.[51]

The Calvinist cheers when this kind of boldness comes from the pulpit, and rightly so. We rejoice that a faithful preacher has reminded us of an essential truth that must never be forgotten. But how easily we do forget this—or at least neglect to apply it—when facing a less theologically informed brother or sister in Christ. How could one who revels in man's spiritual impotence ever become proud? How could a worshiper who sings that he is "a worm" and a "wretch" as "vile" as the thief on the cross ever be smug, especially to a fellow sinner saved by grace?[52]

A few months ago at breakfast, a very mature friend—a much-needed "Paul" in my life and a man who handles his Calvinism well—encouraged me to continue writing this book and gave me some great advice: "Greg, let Calvinism devastate you to the core and bring you to tears." I tried to joke with him about starting a greeting card company with these kinds of non-commercial sentiments, but he would not be deterred. "Greg, I'm serious. Every day I ask God to show me just how lost I would be without him."

This is a man who loves others freely, even those who tease or mock him about his Calvinism. He is in touch with his frailty and helplessness before God. May we all be.

❖ ❖ ❖

Lord, crush my arrogance.

Merciful Father,

Forgive me for my arrogance. How can I ever look down on anyone? If you treated me the way I have treated my own brothers in the faith, I would be lost.

You know my confusion, my spiritual infancy and my complete helplessness, yet you choose to love me. Keep me so close to you that I never for a moment think that I've earned something for my intellectual efforts. Show me that any knowledge I have of you and your ways is woefully lacking and not nearly as rich as my pride would lead me to believe. Show me how small I am so that I would always speak of you the way a child does when he is in awe of his Father. May others see in me a complete distrust of myself and a greater dependence on your grace and mercy alone.

Amen.

Eight

BY SCOFFING AT THE HANG-UPS OTHERS HAVE WITH CALVINISM

I love my church. This affection for my people is not something I take lightly, as if it comes naturally or is a minister's birthright. The pastorate has about as many trying days as it does joyful ones, and vocational ministry has beaten up many of my pastor friends, so I am humbly thankful for this church that loves my wife, my children, and me. I planted Christ Fellowship Church nine years ago, and my people have endured the mixed blessing of being led by a pastor who has now reached age 41 and still has vast stretches of spiritual maturity to traverse. But in God's sweet providence, our church has increased, matured, and done some wonderful things in advancing God's kingdom in our community.

Why do I tell you all of this? Because I think the majority of my congregation doesn't know what Calvinism is. At least not by name.

I won't bore you with the details of how I came to plant a nondenominational church or why the church still has that status today, but it wasn't for lack of trying. I started out in the PCA, but my credo-Baptist impulses got the better of me. I then looked at Sovereign Grace, but I wasn't there in terms of spiritual gifts (close, but not quite). My Reformed Baptist friends beckoned me to come their way, but there were too many differences in philosophy and culture. Acts 29 came along, but my wife kept reminding me, "If you and Driscoll had gone to the same high school, he would have been the cool-guy football captain, and you, Greg, would have been, well, you!" That's Lisa's way of telling me I'm a nerd. Anyway, I love my friends in all of these varied expressions of the Reformed community, but I have ended up in a different section of God's vineyard. In time, I have come to love the ministry of Christ Fellowship Church, and I love the people even more.

The majority of my people are Bible-trusting, Christ-centered disciples who really want to glorify God in their individual lives and in the church. Yet when they hear about Calvinism, many can become suspicious. More often than not, they say something like, "Isn't that about God creating some people for heaven and some people for hell?" Others will shake their heads and protest, "God doesn't make robots. Love is real only when we can choose it." While these are some of the knee-jerk responses to a popular caricature of Calvinism (certainly not the genuine article), that does not make them easy to address. But let me share some good news: if we listen to

By Scoffing at the Hang-ups Others Have with Calvinism

these comments with patience and sincerity, in time we can get a hearing for the beautiful truth of Reformed theology. Sadly, I'm afraid that scores of Christians are never even getting close to giving Calvinists that hearing. Many are turning away prematurely because their objections have been ridiculed.

Face the Emotion

The "out" Calvinist quickly learns the lonely experience of being misunderstood. No matter how much he reads, meditates on Scripture, thinks through objections, and works on helpful illustrations, he is regularly stopped dead in his tracks by intense resistance to his positions. This can get pretty frustrating, and sometimes it is tempting to start railing on the very people we are trying to persuade. I will never forget one young lady telling me, with tears streaming down her cheeks, "Greg, if I believed what you believe about predestination, I would stop being a Christian. I couldn't worship a God like that."

At first I was so shocked I could barely think of a response. Finally I composed myself and managed to smile. And then?

Then I actually mocked her.

"Oh, sure, I see. You should get to decide how things work. Not God. No, he should consult you on your understanding of fairness. Wow, I never knew you were the center of divine wisdom in the universe."

I know you will be amazed to learn that my verbal assault did not make this young lady fall to her knees and beg me to instruct her in the glories of the *Institutes*.

Instead she rolled her eyes, called me rude, and walked away with a silent commitment never to talk with me about this subject again—a commitment she has kept to this day. Much later, I offered as sincere an apology as I could, but as they say, it was too little, too late.

And that is far from my worst true story.

One day I went to lunch at the home of a seminary friend who was an enthusiastic Calvinist, so I assumed his wife was as well. We sat around the table, and she held in her arms a darling one-month-old baby, their first child. In the middle of a wonderful conversation about our testimonies, our sense of call to the ministry, and our family backgrounds, I made a casual comment about election. A moment later it felt like all the air was being sucked out of the room.

The next few seconds were a blur. Trying to change the subject, my friend stammered something barely intelligible. His wife asked me a clarifying question. Stuck on Arrogant Calvinist Autopilot, I responded with some slam on man-centered preaching and the weakness of the Western church. I won't try to recount how things escalated from there, I'll just jump to the climax—my friend's wife holding her newborn daughter inches from my face and screaming, "So if she's not elect, she's going to hell! Isn't that what you're saying, Greg? Say it! Say it!"

Weep with Those Who Weep

I do not know how it happened, but it seems as though we Calvinists have bought into the wisdom of a 1980s slogan for Dry Idea: "Never let 'em see you sweat." It may be a decent tag line for a deodorant, but it's lousy advice for theological dialogue. We are often afraid to say, "I understand. It does seem hard to fathom a God who chooses only some and not everyone," so we argue back. But if we have never stopped to validate the person's emotional concern, it doesn't matter if our retort is 100 percent dead-on right: we have made a huge misstep and almost certainly wasted an opportunity.

Recently an Arminian friend said to me, "Why is it that not one Calvinist has ever told me that he struggles, even for just a second, with the thought of God choosing some and not others?"

When I asked him why this mattered to him so much, his answer hit me right between the eyes: "Because I want to know that you guys aren't Stepford wives! That you actually *feel* something!"

My friend was sincere. He wasn't looking for a chink in the armor of our theological resolve. He wasn't going to say, "Gotcha!" if one of us had a moment of honesty. So at the risk of some gentle reader wanting to revoke my T.U.L.I.P. card, I will admit I came clean: "Yes, at times the thought troubles me."

I told him the truth: there have been nights when I have been up late, when it's quiet and I can think, and I have become pretty emotional at the thought of someone entering into eternal torment. My friend appreciated my candor, and I think this allowed him to consider Calvinism with a little less guardedness. That's a start!

Admitting that someone's emotional hang-up has some merit does not bring down Calvinism like a house

of cards. Hell is in no danger of disappearing if I admit I
have moments of emotional and intellectual discomfort
with it. Such an admission is not a denial of faith or a
rejection of the gospel. To acknowledge that damnation
is beyond awful is to agree with Jesus' assessment of it.

As I mature in Christ, my moments of emotional
strain decrease and I grow in my joy over God's electing love. But I must give others space to work through
their own emotional barriers—the same space most of us
needed when first considering the doctrines of Calvinism.
Why would anyone ever come to love something that
only perplexes or even enrages them? We must explain
compassionately with more of a listening ear than a
lecturing tongue.

Earlier in this book I mentioned R. C. Sproul's
experience of becoming a Calvinist. Let me quote it here
more fully:

> The combination was too much for me. Gerstner,
> Edwards, the New Testament professor, and above
> all the apostle Paul, were too formidable a team for
> me to withstand. The ninth chapter of Romans was
> the clincher. I simply could find no way to avoid the
> apostle's teaching in that chapter. Reluctantly, I sighed
> and surrendered, but with my head, not my heart.
> "OK, I believe this stuff, but I don't have to like it!"

> I soon discovered that God has created us so that the
> heart is supposed to follow the head. I could not, with
> impunity, love something with my head that I hated

in my heart. Once I began to see the cogency of the doctrine and its broader implications, my eyes were opened to the graciousness of grace and to the grand comfort of God's sovereignty. I began to like the doctrine little by little, until it burst upon my soul that the doctrine revealed the depth and the riches of the mercy of God.[53]

I honestly do not know how I would have crossed my final barrier to Reformed theology without Sproul's transparent candor. Because he was willing to admit that he was initially a reluctant and then a committed Calvinist, I felt that maybe I could make the transition as well. Sproul did not mock the emotional reticence that often comes with embracing Calvinism. It was as if he stared it square in the eye and said, "It's okay. I understand." I'm so glad that he did.

What if we all stopped mocking other believers who disagree with Calvinism? What would happen if we simply said, "Tell me more about that. I really want to understand where you're coming from. I know how much you love the Lord, and I respect your struggle. Let's talk about it." Imagine if the first words that came to mind when people thought of Calvinists were "gentle" and "empathetic" instead of "scholarly," "argumentative," and "arrogant."

Is it really that hard to be gentle and empathetic when people are struggling with something as significant as how God saves sinners? We live in a massively choice-driven culture. People make millions of decisions in their lifetimes, and most Christians naturally consider their salvation experience a decision—a big one, but a decision all the same. Indeed, echoing the example of Scripture, evangelistic messages are nearly always couched in the language of decision. Those who have freely chosen a spouse, a school, or a fantasy football team often think—quite understandably—that they have also chosen a Savior. [54]

I say all this to point out that people don't change paradigms overnight—*especially* not Christians. That's because all Christians know (or least sense) that they have already undergone the greatest transformation anyone ever can—yes, even greater than the change from Arminianism to Calvinism. It makes sense that Christians who have genuinely encountered the living God in the Bible can have great difficulty coming to terms with the possibility that they might still be "missing it" in some significant way.

As one who ministers mostly to those who don't see themselves as Reformed, I ask you to trust me when I say that letting go of a worldview can be like letting go of a loved one. For the typical evangelical in the West, what helps him or her make sense of the world is a kind of unexamined "Arminianism lite," absorbed by osmosis from the broader Christian culture, tainted as that culture is by humanism and postmodernism and whatever else. For many of these genuine believers, this perspective *is* Christianity, however vague and ill-formed it may seem from our side of the theological fence. They love it and feel they need it. To let go of something you have cherished in this way often requires a period of grieving.

Teach with Grace and Wisdom

As a Calvinist, I fully believe that the system of doctrine I espouse is indeed what the Bible teaches. However, because the false baggage that has been heaped upon Calvinism's reputation can actually hinder the process of getting a better grip on Scripture, my congregation is learning the content of Calvinism without some of the official labels.

I am hardly the first pastor to teach Calvinism "anonymously" simply by teaching God's Word. But I have learned that when my people see what the *Bible* says about God, sin, and salvation, they are more and more open to adjusting their prior conceptions of what it means to be saved. I believe this is the key to bringing Christians out of their Arminianism (conscious or unconscious, examined or unexamined), and into what Spurgeon simply called a nickname for the gospel. We must help people see what the Bible actually says.

When we are encouraging someone to see more clearly what it means to be diligent in prayer or to love one's spouse or to be honest in business, we are engaged in a process of teaching, not an act of discipline. We are trying to show, hopefully with grace and kindness, what the Scriptures teach on a given subject. Why should our conversations about Calvinism be any different? All we are trying to do is unpack Scripture.

Let's accept the fact that Calvinism's reputation has been falsely tainted and that few of the Christians who oppose it actually understand its tenets. Let's accept the reality that our efforts will meet with opposition. If we believe that the heart of Calvinism is simply an accurate restatement of the gospel, then opposition based on misunderstanding should not surprise us—distortion of the gospel has been a principal goal of the enemy from the beginning.

All we need to do is remember that the Bible teaches God's sovereignty in salvation. We can teach the tenets of Calvinism (by name or not) the same way we would any other topic. Scripture leaves with me no doubt as to the tone I must take when talking about his Word:

> And the Lord's servant must *not be quarrelsome* but *kind to everyone*, able to teach, patiently enduring evil (2 Timothy 2:24).

> But in your hearts regard Christ the Lord as holy, always being prepared to make a defense to anyone who asks you for a reason for the hope that is in you; yet do it with *gentleness and respect* (1 Peter 3:15).

> But we were gentle among you, like a *nursing mother* taking care of her own children (1 Thessalonians 2:7).

When we dispense sacred truths in any capacity—in a classroom setting, during a casual conversation, or at the request of an unbeliever—we are to be kind and gentle in our manner. Alexander Strauch, who literally wrote the book on church leadership, accurately contrasts a good teacher with a bad one:

> Good teachers are approachable and easy to talk to;
> they are not irritable, defensive, or quick to argue
> with people who disagree …. We must not lose our
> temper, scold our students, yell at them, or seek
> revenge because they offend us …. Angry preachers
> and teachers generate fear and stifle the spirit of
> inquiry, especially in children and adolescents.[55]

I have great remorse about the number of people that
might say that they were at some point afraid to talk about
predestination and election with me. If people did not feel
at ease in my presence then I have done a great disservice.
Let me say it more bluntly: I have sinned. May God grant
me and every Calvinist who falters in this area the grace to
commend Calvinism with a gentle, merciful spirit.

✳ ✳ ✳

Lord, help me love those who disagree.

God of all grace,
    You have reconciled me to yourself. And you have
also reconciled me to my brother in Christ, even the
one who does not agree with me. Forgive me, Lord, for
mocking that precious soul, the one you sent your Son
to die for. Show me, Lord, your love of him and how
much you want me to love him with kindness, gentle-
ness, and respect. He is your child, Lord, so please
increase my love for him. Keep me from pettiness and
pride and help me speak to him in love and sincerity.

Your word is truth, Lord, and I trust that your word will be sufficient to change all of our hearts without me bullying others to make it happen. Just as you were patient with me, teach me to be patient with all of my brothers and sisters in Christ until we all grow up into maturity. For the glory of your Son.

Amen.

AFTERWORD

No Book Can Save Calvinism

I do not imagine for a moment that I have given the final word on how Calvinism should be handled or presented. If anything, this is a tiny drop in a huge bucket. I have heard John Piper say that in recent years he has come to have small expectations of individual sermons, and I'm sure the same applies to little books. If this book has sparked just one thought that helps you want to be a better Calvinist, then I feel I have done my job.

The doctrines of grace are revitalizing many churches and movements within Christendom. May God use this resurgence to purify the church and make his servants more humble and joyful. My hope is that you have read this book because you want to handle your own Calvinism well. If you have children, I pray that they will be able to use your life as a model for Calvinism well lived and well applied. If you have other thoughts on how to avoid killing Calvinism, please share them with me. Like you, I want to finish well and commend this God-centered faith to future generations.

Contact me at **GregDutcher.com**.

APPENDIX

The Calvinist's Favorite Flower: T.U.L.I.P.

Total Depravity

Sin controls every part of man. He is spiritually dead and blind, and unable to obey, believe, or repent. He continually sins, for his nature is completely evil.

Unconditional Election

God chose the elect solely on the basis of his free grace, not anything in them. He has a special love for the elect. God left the rest to be damned for their sins.

Limited Atonement

Christ died especially for the elect, and paid a definite price for them that guaranteed their salvation.

Irresistible Grace

Saving grace is irresistible, for the Holy Spirit is invincible and intervenes in man's heart. He sovereignly gives the new birth, faith, and repentance to the elect.

Perseverance of the Saints

God preserves all the elect and causes them to persevere in faith and obedience to the end. None are continually backslidden or finally lost.

Endnotes

1. I make no pretense: this is a book by a Calvinist for other Calvinists. I have not included a "What is Calvinism" section, for others have offered excellent treatments on that subject. For the purposes of this book, I use the words *Calvinism* and *Calvinists* as they are used popularly: generally speaking, this theological perspective assumes God's sovereignty in salvation and is summarized in the famous TULIP acrostic. While such persons engage in worthwhile intramural debates on ecclesiology, eschatology, and church polity, this book assumes a broad understanding of "the Reformed" from the most diehard high-liturgy brother in the OPC to the hand-lifting, foot-tapping brother at a Sovereign Grace church.

2. Charles Spurgeon, *Spurgeon's Sovereign Grace Sermons* (Still Waters Revival Books, 1990), 170

3. Colin Hansen's movement-defining article, "Young, Restless, and Reformed" (Christianity Today, September 22, 2006), and his follow-up book of the same title (Crossway, 2008) amply illustrate the success of the young Reformed movement. Books, websites, conferences, and a line of well-known authors and speakers have helped shape a culture that simply did not exist a generation ago.

4. R. C. Sproul, *Chosen By God,* rev. ed. (Tyndale House, 1986), 4

5. Kevin DeYoung, "Why I Am a Calvinist," *Christian Research Journal* 32.3 (2009), http://www.equip.org/PDF/JAVP3231.pdf.

6. Charles Haddon Spurgeon, "A Defense of Calvinism," accessed April 20, 2012, www.spurgeon.org/calvinis.htm

7. See http://www.reformationtheology.com/2006/06/quotes_to_ponder.php

8. Suggested reading on the life of a mind like this: Mark Noll's *The Scandal of the Evangelical Mind* (Eerdmans,1994), John Piper's *Think: The Life of the Mind and the Love of God* (Crossway, 2010), and James Sire's *Habits of the Mind: Intellectual Life As a Christian Calling* (InterVarsity, 2000).

9. See Matthew 4:1-11. See also Mark 1:24 where the demons are the first to recognize Jesus' identity.

10. James Edwards, *The Gospel According to Mark* (Eerdmans, 2002), 113

11. Thomas Brooks, "An Ark for All God's Noahs," *The Complete*

Works of Thomas Brooks, Vol. 2, Ed. Rev. Alexander Balloch Grosart (Edinburgh: James Nichol, 1866), 27

12. Charles Spurgeon, *Morning and Evening* (Hendrickson, 1996), 346

13. John Piper, *Seeing and Savoring Jesus Christ,* (Crossway, 2003), 29

14. See the classic summation of incommunicable attributes in Louis Berkhof, *Manual of Christian Doctrine* (Eerdmans, 1939), 62–65.

15. I recommend reading Piper's whole sermon "Glorification: Conformed to Christ for the Supremacy of Christ," August 11, 2002, http://www.desiringgod.org/resource-library/sermons/glorification-conformed-to-christ-for-the-supremacy-of-christ.

16. By "elect" here, I mean all Christians—not merely those who embrace Calvinism.

17. Spurgeon, *Morning and Evening,* 398

18.. I am indebted to Josh Harris for this perfect label.

19. See Michael Horton's *For Calvinism* (Zondervan, 2011) and James White's "How to Avoid Cage-Stage-itis" (last updated September 13, 2007, http://www.aomin.org/aoblog/index.php?itemid=2269&catid=4).

20. Thanks to my friend Doug Dempsey for this phrase.

21. John Piper, "Why Are Calvinists So Negative?" May 21, 2008, http://www.desiringgod.org/resource-library/ask-pastor-john/why-are-calvinists-so-negative.

22. Thomas Boston, "The Purpose of God's Decrees," accessed June 23, 2011, http://www.puritansermons.com/boston/bost6.htm, emphasis added

23. I applaud John Piper's balanced Calvinism here. No one is about to revoke his 5-Point-Card (in fact, he holds to 7 points of Calvinism!), but he has served the church so effectively by reminding us about the end game of God's sovereignty in our salvation: glory. See his *Seeing and Savoring Jesus Christ* (Crossway, 2004), 16.

24. This is exactly what Paul does in Romans 11:33-36, ending three chapters of the most exhaustive treatment of God's sovereignty found anywhere in the Bible.

25. Anonymous lyricist, c. 1904, "I Sought the Lord," *Trinity Hymnal* (Great Commission Publications, 1987), 397

26. John Owen, *The Glory of Christ* (Moody Press, 1980), 69

27. John Wesley, "Free Grace" *Readings in Historical Theology*, Ed. Robert F. Lay (Kregel, 2009), 327

28. See Iain Murray's *Wesley and Men Who Followed* (Carlisle, PA: Banner of Truth, 2003) and Mark Noll's *The Rise of Evangelicalism: The Age of Edwards, Whitefield and the Wesleys* (Westmont, IL: InterVarsity, 2010).

29. See chapter six for more on this subject (my own sinful arrogance could provide enough material for three books!)

30. John Piper, "How to Teach and Preach Calvinism," July 4, 1998, http://www.desiringgod.org/resource-library/articles/how-to-teach-and-preach-calvinism.

31. J. I. Packer, *Evangelism and the Sovereignty of God* (InterVarsity Press, 1991), 99-100

32. See, for example, http://www.billhybels.org and http://www.willowcreek.com/international/affiliates.asp and http://www.willowcreekglobalsummit.com/about.asp.

33. Tim Keller serves as Senior Pastor of Redeemer Presbyterian Church in New York City, and he has written *The Reason for God* and *The Prodigal God*, among other excellent titles. Keller has a similarly kind and humble affect that I've always found appealing while certainly espousing Reformed theology.

34. Hybels and the seeker-sensitive movement he helped build has done some real damage to both the psyche and the mission of many churches. Our love affair with entertainment and pragmatism has been a direct result of the Willow Creek model so prevalent in American evangelicalism. But I do not think that it *logically* follows that the leaders within this movement have nothing to share with other believers.

35. Ken Sande, *The Peacemaker* (Baker, 2004), 171

36. Bob Smietana's "C. S. Lewis Superstar" (with additional reporting by Rebecca Barnes, *Christianity Today*, November 23, 2005, http://www.christianitytoday.com/ct/2005/december/9.28.html) details the 50-year evangelical infatuation with Lewis.

37. J. I. Packer, "Still Surprised by Lewis," *Christianity Today*, September 7, 1998, http://www.christianitytoday.com/ct/1998/september7/8ta054.html.

38. A letter from George Whitefield to John Wesley, last accessed July 21, 2011, http://www.spurgeon.org/~phil/wesley.htm

39. Some of my Calvinist friends agree with Pastor Blight at least by believing in a premillenial, pre-tribulation rapture. In fact, John MacArthur would tell me that my disagreement on that point makes me an inconsistent Calvinist. See his *The Second Coming: Signs of Christ's Return and the End of the Age* (Crossway, 1999) for more.

40. The appendix, "The Calvinist's Favorite Flower: T.U.L.I.P.," summarizes the main points.

41. Study Bibles are a great analogy. I love putting good study Bibles into the hands of new believers, but I say, "The words under the line on the bottom of every page are comments from Bible scholars. They are helpful and should serve you in your Bible reading. But they are not on par with Scripture, and they are always subordinate to what the Scripture actually says."

42. God has never relaxed his standard of perfect obedience as laid down in Leviticus 18:5. So when Jesus comes he commits himself to a life of perfect obedience to the Father. "Although he was a son, he learned obedience through what he suffered. And being made perfect, he became the source of eternal salvation to all who obey him" (Hebrews 5:8–9).

43. There are various ways to grapple with the idea of false teachers being "bought" by Christ. 1) Some may argue that the false teachers are indeed Christians, but the verses that seemingly describe their future judgment make that interpretation difficult. 2) Others might say "bought" can be used in a different sense than Christ's redeeming work on the cross. 3) My own suspicion is that Peter is being sarcastic: the false teachers *profess* to be "bought" by Christ, but their lives show the absurd nature of that profession. Who would live contrary to the one who allegedly "owns" him? Whatever one's view is of this passage, though, the verse must be wrestled with honestly. We cannot say, "It doesn't matter since I'm a Calvinist."

44. I believe that D. A. Carson's *The Difficult Doctrine of the Love of God* (Wheaton, IL: Crossway, 2000) should be mandatory reading for every Calvinist. Carson masterfully shows how rich and nuanced the love of God is in Scripture. His thoughts on the relationship between God's universal love for all and his electing love for his own are outstanding.

45. Charles Spurgeon, "The Last Words of Christ on the Cross," last accessed October 14, 2011, http://www.spurgeongems.org/vols43-45/chs2644.pdf

46. *Matthew Henry's Complete Commentary on the Whole Bible*, complete and unabridged in one volume (Hendrickson, 1996), 457

47. Joe Thorn, interview by Ed Stetzer, *Ed Stetzer: The LifeWay Research Blog*, September 14, 2011, http://www.edstetzer.com/2011/09/joe-thorn-and-fake-calvinists.html

48. The eminent biographer Iain Murray wrote an outstanding biography of one of Arminianism's leading men: *Wesley and Men Who Followed* is a fascinating read. Murray received a tidal wave of criticism for the book, as though writing it signaled that he was turning his back on his own staunchly Reformed credentials and on the Calvinist cause in general. If Whitefield paid tribute to Wesley's exceptional life, shouldn't contemporary Calvinists as well?

49. Jonathan Edwards, "Revival of Religion in New England," *The Works of President Edwards, in Four Volumes*, vol. III (Leavitt & Allen, 1851), 355

50. John Piper, "Why Are Calvinists So Negative?" May 21, 2008, http://www.desiringgod.org/resource-library/ask-pastor-john/why-are-calvinists-so-negative

51. Charles Spurgeon, "Human Inability," delivered March 7, 1858, last accessed November 18, 2011, http://www.spurgeon.org/sermons/0182.htm

52. Thank God for the sobering, pride-crushing words of the old hymns: the singer calls himself a worm in "O Sacred Head Now Wounded," a wretch in "Amazing Grace," and vile as the thief crucified with Jesus in "There Is A Fountain Filled with Blood."

53. R. C. Sproul, *Chosen by God*, rev. ed. (Tyndale, 1986), 4–5

54. Of course, I reject the caricature that Calvinists do not see the will involved in salvation. I affirm with my Reformed brethren that will is free but is free according to its nature. My argument here is simply intended to "track" with a non-Calvinist when discussing his concerns over "free will."

55. Alexander Strauch, *Leading with Love* (Lewis and Roth, 2006), 130–131

Who Am I?
Identity in Christ

by Jerry Bridges

Jerry Bridges unpacks Scripture to give the Christian eight clear, simple, interlocking answers to one of the most essential questions of life.

"Jerry Bridges' gift for simple but deep spiritual communication is fully displayed in this warm-hearted, biblical spelling out of the Christian's true identity in Christ."

> **J.I. Packer, Theological Editor, ESV Study Bible; author, Knowing God, A Quest for Godliness, Concise Theology**

"I know of no one better prepared than Jerry Bridges to write *Who Am I?* He is a man who knows who he is in Christ and he helps us to see succinctly and clearly who we are to be. Thank you for another gift to the Church of your wisdom and insight in this book."

> **R.C. Sproul, founder, chairman, president, Ligonier Ministries; executive editor, Tabletalk magazine; general editor, The Reformation Study Bible**

"*Who Am I?* answers one of the most pressing questions of our time in clear gospel categories straight from the Bible. This little book is a great resource to ground new believers and remind all of us of what God has made us through faith in Jesus. Thank the Lord for Jerry Bridges, who continues to provide the warm, clear, and biblically balanced teaching that has made him so beloved to this generation of Christians."

> **Richard D. Phillips, Senior Minister, Second Presbyterian Church, Greenville, SC**

Licensed to Kill
A Field Manual for Mortifying Sin

by Brian G. Hedges

**Your soul is a war zone.
Know your enemy.
Learn to fight.**

"A faithful, smart, Word-centered guide."
– *Wes Ward, Revive Our Hearts*

"Are there things you hate that you end up doing anyway? Have you tried to stop sinning in certain areas of your life, only to face defeat over and over again? If you're ready to get serious about sin patterns in your life—ready to put sin to death instead of trying to manage it—this book outlines the only strategy that works. This is a book I will return to and regularly recommend to others."
> *Bob Lepine, Co-Host,* **FamilyLife Today**

"Brian Hedges shows the importance of fighting the sin that so easily entangles us and robs us of our freedom, by fleeing to the finished work of Christ every day. Well done!"
> *Tullian Tchividjian, Coral Ridge Presbyterian Church; author,* **Jesus + Nothing = Everything**

"Rather than aiming at simple moral reformation, *Licensed to Kill* aims at our spiritual transformation. Like any good field manual, this one focuses on the most critical information regarding our enemy, and gives practical instruction concerning the stalking and killing of sin. This is a theologically solid and helpfully illustrated book that holds out the gospel confidence of sin's ultimate demise."
> *Joe Thorn, pastor and author,* **Note to Self: The Discipline of Preaching to Yourself**

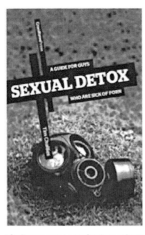

Sexual Detox
A Guide for Guys Who Are Sick of Porn

by Tim Challies

"In an age when sex is worshiped as a god, a little book like this can go a long way to helping men overcome sexual addiction."
  –Pastor Mark Driscoll
  Mars Hill Church
  Acts 29

"Online pornography is not just a problem for Christian men; it is THE problem. Many men, young and old, in our churches need *Sexual Detox*. Challies offers practical, doable and, above all, gospel-centered hope for men. I want every man I serve and all the guys on our staff to read this book."
  Tedd Tripp, Pastor, and author of Shepherding a Child's Heart

"Tim Challies strikes just the right balance in this necessary work. His assessment of the sexual epidemic in our culture is sober but not without hope. His advice is practical but avoids a checklist mentality. His discussion of sexual sin is frank without being inappropriate. This book will be a valuable resource."
  Kevin DeYoung, Pastor and author

"Thank God for using Tim to articulate simply and unashamedly the truth about sex amidst a culture of permissiveness."
  Ben Zobrist, Tampa Bay Rays

"*Sexual Detox* is just what we need. It is clear, honest, and biblical, written with a tone that is knowing but kind, exhortative but gracious, realistic but determined. We have been given by Tim Challies a terrific resource for fighting sin and exalting Christ.
  Owen Strachan, Boyce College

Getting Back in the Race
The Cure for Backsliding

by Joel R. Beeke

Backsliding is the worst thing that can happen to anyone claiming faith in Jesus.

Find out why. Learn the diagnosis. Experience the cure.

"This book is a masterpiece, and I do not say that lightly. This excellent work, so helpfully spiced with quotations from the Puritans, needs to be read over and over again. I heartily commend it."
Martin Holdt, Pastor; editor, Reformation Africa South

"Joel Beeke's characteristic clarity, biblical fidelity, and unflinching care as to detail and pastoral wisdom is obvious on every page. This book is an honest and sometimes chilling exposition of the seriousness of backsliding; at the same time, it unfailingly breathes the air of grace and hope. Timely and judicious."
Derek W. H. Thomas, First Presbyterian Church, Columbia, SC; Editorial Director, Alliance of Confessing Evangelicals

"'Don't settle for being a spiritual shrimp,' argues Dr. Beeke. The pity is that too many modern Christians are opting for shrimpishly small degrees of grace. Indwelling sin drags the careless believer down into guilty backsliding. This book is a prescription for the believer who feels his guilt."
Maurice Roberts, former editor, Banner of Truth *magazine*

"Dr. Beeke outlines the best means of bringing balm and healing to the backslidden soul. Highly recommended."
Michael Haykin, Professor, Southern Baptist Theo. Sem.

Grieving, Hope and Solace
When a Loved One Dies in Christ
by Albert N. Martin

**There is comfort for the grief.
There are answers to the questions.
The Bible does offer hope, solace,
healing, and confidence.**

**Pastor Albert Martin has been
there.**

"This tender book by a much-loved pastor, written after the death of
his beloved wife, offers comfort to those in tears. A rare guidebook to
teach us how to grieve with godliness, it is relevant to us all — if not for
today, then no doubt for tomorrow."
Maurice Roberts, former editor, Banner of Truth *magazine*

"Albert N. Martin is a seasoned pastor, skilled teacher, and gifted writer
who has given us a priceless treasure in this book. All who read these
pages will, unquestionably, be pointed to Christ and find themselves
greatly helped."
Steve Lawson, Christ Fellowship Baptist Church, Mobile, AL

"Like turning the corner and being met by a glorious moonrise, or
discovering a painter or musician who touches us in the deepest
recesses of our being–this little book by Pastor Al Martin has been
such an experience for me. Whether you are a pastor or counselor,
one who is experiencing the pangs of grief, or a member of the
church who wants to be useful to others, you need to read this book."
Joseph Pipa, President, Greenville Presbyterian Theo. Sem.

"Personal tenderness and biblical teaching in a sweet book of comfort. Buy it and give it away, but make sure to get a copy for yourself."
Dr. Joel R. Beeke, President, Puritan Reformed Theo. Sem.

The Organized Heart
A Woman's Guide to Conquering Chaos

by Staci Eastin

**Disorganized?
You don't need more rules, the
latest technique, or a new gadget.**

**This book will show you a different,
better way. A way grounded in the
grace of God.**

"Staci Eastin packs a gracious punch, full of insights about our
disorganized hearts and lives, immediately followed by the balm of
gospel-shaped hopes. This book is ideal for accountability partners
and small groups."

> *Carolyn McCulley, blogger, filmmaker, author of* Radical Wom-
> anhood *and* Did I Kiss Marriage Goodbye?

"Unless we understand the spiritual dimension of productivity, our
techniques will ultimately backfire. Find that dimension here. Encouraging and uplifting rather than guilt-driven, this book can help
women who want to be more organized but know that adding a new
method is not enough."

> *Matt Perman, Director of Strategy at Desiring God, blogger,
> author of the forthcoming book,* What's Best Next: How the
> Gospel Transforms the Way You Get Things Done

"Organizing a home can be an insurmountable challenge for a woman. The Organized Heart makes a unique connection between idols
of the heart and the ability to run a well-managed home. This is not
a how-to. Eastin looks at sin as the root problem of disorganization.
She offers a fresh new approach and one I recommend, especially to
those of us who have tried all the other self-help models and failed."

> *Aileen Challies, Mom of three, and wife of blogger, author, and
> pastor Tim Challies*

"But God..."
The Two Words at the Heart of the Gospel

by Casey Lute

Just two words.
Understand their use in Scripture,
and you will never be the same.

"Rock-solid theology packaged in an engaging and accessible form."
– Louis Tullo, Sight Regained blog

"Keying off of nine occurrences of "But God" in the English Bible, Casey Lute ably opens up Scripture in a manner that is instructive, edifying, encouraging, and convicting. This little book would be useful in family or personal reading, or as a gift to a friend. You will enjoy Casey's style, you will have a fresh view of some critical Scripture, and your appreciation for God's mighty grace will be deepened."
Dan Phillips, Pyromaniacs blog, author of The World-Tilting Gospel (forthcoming from Kregel)

"A refreshingly concise, yet comprehensive biblical theology of grace that left this reader more in awe of the grace of God."
Aaron Armstrong, BloggingTheologically. com

""Casey Lute reminds us that nothing is impossible with God, that we must always reckon with God, and that God brings life out of death and joy out of sorrow."
Thomas R. Schreiner, Professor of New Testament Interpretation, The Southern Baptist Theological Seminary

"A mini-theology that will speak to the needs of every reader of this small but powerful book. Read it yourself and you will be blessed. Give it to a friend and you will be a blessing."
William Varner, Prof. of Biblical Studies, The Master's College